How to Be Assertive in Any Situation

SECOND EDITION

SUE HADFIELD AND GILL HASSON

Harlow, England • London • New York • Boston • San Francisco • Toronto • Sydney • Auckland • Singapore • Hong Kong
Tokyo • Seoul • Taipei • New Delhi • Cape Town • São Paulo • Mexico City • Madrid • Amsterdam • Munich • Paris • Milan

PEARSON EDUCATION LIMITED
Edinburgh Gate
Harlow CM20 2JE
Tel: +44 (0)1279 623623
Fax: +44 (0)1279 431059
Website: www.pearsoned.co.uk

First published 2010
Second edition published 2014 (print and electronic)

ISBN: 978-0-273-78522-4 (print)
        978-0-273-78873-7 (PDF)
        978-0-273-78874-4 (ePub)
        978-1-292-00664-2 (eText)

British Library Cataloguing-in-Publication Data
A catalogue record for this book is available from the British Library.

Library of Congress Cataloging-in-Publication Data
Hadfield, Sue.
  How to be assertive in any situation / Sue Hadfield And Gill Hasson.-- Second edition.
    pages cm
  Includes index.
  ISBN 978-0-273-78522-4 (pbk.)
  1. Assertiveness (Psychology) 2. Interpersonal communication. 3. Interpersonal relations.
  I. Hasson, Gill. II. Title.
  BF575.A85H33 2014
  158.2--dc23
                        2013037763

10 9 8 7 6 5 4 3 2 1
17 16 15 14 13

Cover design by Two Associates
Typeset in 9.5/13pt ITC Giovanni Std by 30
Printed and bound in Great Britain by Henry Ling Ltd., at the Dorest Press, Dorchester, Dorset

NOTE THAT ANY PAGE CROSS REFERNCES REFER TO THE PRINT EDITION

Ho

Z935714

Assertive in

Community Learning & Libraries
Cymuned Ddysgu a Llyfrgelloedd

This item should be returned or renewed by the last date stamped below.

Newport
CITY COUNCIL
CYNGOR DINAS
Casnewydd

Newport Library and
Information Service
John Frost Square
Newport
South Wales NP20 1PA

17 DEC 2022

1 5 FEB 2014

19/1/23

0 2 AUG 2014

1 8 OCT 2014

2 3 APR 2019

2 4 APR 2019

PEARSON

At Pearson, we believe in learning – all kinds of learning for all kinds of people. Whether it's at home, in the classroom or in the workplace, learning is the key to improving our life chances.

That's why we're working with leading authors to bring you the latest thinking and best practices, so you can get better at the things that are important to you. You can learn on the page or on the move, and with content that's always crafted to help you understand quickly and apply what you've learned.

If you want to upgrade your personal skills or accelerate your career, become a more effective leader or more powerful communicator, discover new opportunities or simply find more inspiration, we can help you make progress in your work and life.

Pearson is the world's leading learning company. Our portfolio includes the Financial Times and our education business, Pearson International.

Every day our work helps learning flourish, and wherever learning flourishes, so do people.

To learn more, please visit us at **www.pearson.com/uk**

Contents

About the authors

Sue Hadfield and **Gill Hasson** are both teachers and joint authors of *Bounce – use the power of resilience to live the life you want* (Pearson Education, 2009).

Sue Hadfield taught English in comprehensive schools for 20 years where she also ran courses and workshops on assertiveness for the students, staff and parents. She has spent the last ten years teaching adults – assertiveness, creative writing, study skills and career and personal development – at the University of Sussex and for community groups. She believes that being assertive is an essential part of leading a happy, successful and fulfilling life. Sue is the author of *Brilliant Positive Thinking* (2012) and *Change One Thing* (2013).

Gill Hasson works with people from diverse backgrounds and situations. Her key motivation is her belief in the ability of people to positively change their way of thinking – about life, other people and themselves. As well as delivering adult education courses in personal development in Brighton, she teaches study skills at the University of Sussex. Gill delivers training in child and adolescent development to pre-school, youth and social workers and parents.

You can contact Gill and Sue at www.makingsenseof.com

Authors' acknowledgements

We would like to thank our families, friends, students and work colleagues for their interest and enthusiasm – and for allowing us to use their stories as case studies. Extra thanks to all our students who have put the methods described in this book into practice and then told us about the transformation of their lives and their relationships.

Many thanks also to Sam Jackson, Melanie Carter, Lucy Carter and Eloise Cook for their interest, encouragement and direction.

Publisher's acknowledgements

We are grateful to the following for permission to reproduce copyright material:

Extract on pages 68–9. Interview with Rosa Parks from scholastic. com teacher website. Copyright by Scholastic Inc. Reprinted by permission of Scholastic Inc.

In some instances we have been unable to trace the owners of copyright material, and we would appreciate any information that would enable us to do so.

Introduction

When we wrote the first edition of *How to Be Assertive* we wanted to write a practical book on assertiveness for those students who weren't able to attend our classes. This first edition has shown us just how universal is the interest in this issue; *How to Be Assertive* has been translated into 15 languages since it was first published in September 2010. It is interesting to consider that, despite cultural and religious differences in countries such as India, Germany, China, Norway and Russia, what we all have in common is a desire to live a fulfilling life that is not limited by fear and anxiety.

We have found that sometimes people are confused about what the word 'assertiveness' means: being assertive doesn't just mean standing up for yourself, it also means taking the other person's feelings into account and often encouraging them to be assertive themselves. An assertive person is still kind and considerate; your personality doesn't change when you become assertive – you just become more like the person you always wanted to be.

When you are assertive your life is easier because you can stop worrying – you know that you can deal with things as they happen. You are no longer saying yes because you are afraid of what will happen if you say no; you are more authentically yourself. Being able to express your opinion without worrying about whether people won't like what you say means you feel more self-confident and happier. A confident, calm and assertive person is also kind and considerate.

Since the success of the first edition we have received many emails from fans of the book with helpful suggestions about situations that they haven't found easy to resolve. We have taken these ideas on board and included additional material on the importance of personal values – that when you respond to others and make decisions that correspond with your values it is easier to be assertive. And we have added a new chapter with information on being assertive at meetings.

In this second edition of the book we have responded to people who have asked us for specific help in difficult situations. There are two other new chapters. 'How to help others to be assertive' shows how you can help other people be more assertive with **you** and with **other people**. It explains how you can help them to be honest, open and direct about how they feel and what they do and don't want in their dealings with **others**.

The other new chapter, 'How to deal with difficult people', shows how you can deal effectively with those people who don't seem to fit any of the usual assertiveness examples. For instance, the kind of people who wear you down with their negativity, those who drive you mad with their neediness and those who sulk with you for days on end.

Whenever you are faced with a potential confrontation or difficult situation, ask yourself what you want the outcome to be. If your answer is 'I'd like them to realise … ' or 'I'd like them to understand … ', or even 'I'd like them to change … ', then you don't have much chance of success. One of the first lessons in assertiveness is that you can't change another person, or make them say the things you want them to say or be the way you want them to be. You can only change your own responses and the way you react to them.

"I wanted to change the world. But I have found that the only thing one can be sure of changing is oneself.**"**

Aldous Huxley

For details of our assertiveness courses and one-to-one assertiveness sessions, you can contact us via our website: www. makingsenseof.com

Introduction from previous edition

Many a major social and political change has started with one person deciding to assert themselves.

Throughout history, men and women have stood up to express what they would or wouldn't accept, and how they wanted themselves and others to be treated. They did not let a fear of conflict silence them and were prepared to take the consequences of their actions.

On 1 December 1955, 42-year-old Rosa Parks decided to take a seat reserved only for white people, on a bus in Alabama. She refused the driver's demand to give up her seat for a white passenger. Her action (preceded by a similar refusal from 15-year-old Claudette Colvin) prompted the Montgomery bus boycott and ended segregation between white people and black people on buses in the southern States of America.

As a result of witnessing the deaths of three children on a Belfast estate in August 1976, 33-year-old Betty Williams, along with Mairead Maguire, the children's aunt, began campaigning for peace. The two women founded the Peace People Organisation, a movement of Catholics and Protestants working to end sectarian violence in Northern Ireland. Williams and Maguire were joint recipients of the Nobel Peace Prize in 1977.

Women such as these and men such as Nelson Mandela and Gandhi are just a few examples of people who have stuck to the principles of assertive communication and behaviour. They stood up for themselves and for others.

They may not always have been confident of success, and often they may have been anxious about the outcome, but this didn't stop them from taking action. They were able to make change occur through behaving assertively.

You can do it too! You might not want to change **the** world but you can make changes in **your** world.

What would it mean to you if you were more assertive?

You would have the ability to express your feelings constructively, be open to others about what you do and don't want. If you were more assertive, you would maximise the chances of getting the relationships you want, the job you want, the friends you want and the life you want. You could be more confident, less frustrated and less anxious. You would be able to help other people assert themselves.

In our work as teachers of personal and career development, we are often struck by the extent to which many people are held back by their lack of self-confidence and ability to deal with other people assertively. We have written a book that will help them and you.

How will it help? Quite simply, by helping you to understand clearly what assertiveness is, how to be assertive and how to help people assert themselves with you. In Chapter 1 we start by looking at what assertiveness is and is not. You will learn that there are advantages and disadvantages to behaving assertively and unassertively. No one is assertive or unassertive all the time – we explain why and when it is easy and when it is difficult to be assertive. The quiz in this chapter will help you identify in which situations and circumstances you could be more assertive. You will see that your self-esteem, expectations, values and rights all play a part in your ability to be assertive.

Before you take those first steps to becoming more assertive, you will learn, in Chapter 2, that changing the way you behave and communicate is part of a process – a series of steps. One of the most important of those steps is being clear and specific about what aspects of your behaviour and communication you want to change and be more assertive in. When you have completed the quiz at the end of Chapter 1, you will already have a good idea of what those aspects are.

It is important to know that, as with any changes, there will be ups and downs.

However, you must not let setbacks undermine your confidence and determination to change your behaviour and become more assertive. You will feel more confident about being assertive if you identify your skills and strengths and the positive people in your life that will support you in your efforts to become more assertive.

Of course, body language has an impact on your ability to be assertive, but you will also discover that an ability to give and receive compliments goes a long way in helping establish a positive approach.

By this point in the book you will have learnt what assertiveness is and is not and you will have recognised in which aspects of your behaviour and communication you could be more assertive. You will have also understood the importance of acting from a position of strength. But there are two important things you need before you take action: you need to choose to be assertive and you need to know how to be assertive. Chapter 3 will show you how: you will learn how to tell other people what you do and do not want.

This includes identifying how you feel and being clear and direct. It includes listening to and accepting other people's views but at the same time asserting your own rights. It includes knowing when to stand your ground and when to compromise and negotiate. Finally, you will learn the importance of taking responsibility and not blaming other people for the outcomes of your interactions.

In Chapter 4 the focus is very much on your reaction to other people: how to be assertive when you want to give criticism or have to take criticism. You will understand why you may react badly to criticism and we will discuss ways of dealing with it assertively. We will examine the reasons why some people bully, and suggest useful ways of responding to the bully at home and at work.

Be patient with yourself as you learn the new skills. Becoming more assertive takes time, genuine intention and courage.

It may feel difficult to imagine yourself being assertive. To help you, in Part 2 we look at situations where people are finding it hard to be assertive – typically, at work, with friends and family. You will also learn how to assert yourself at an interview and when buying products and services.

The last chapter is about decision making. The ability to make good decisions in your life is all part of learning to be assertive. This chapter explores the reasons why you may, at times, be frozen with indecision and examines the mistakes that people often make to avoid making decisions. There is clear guidance about the decision-making process and you are taken through the six logical steps to becoming a more decisive person.

For each chapter there are sample assertive phrases and actions for you to try out and you will find a useful list of assertive responses in Appendix 1.

Asserting yourself will not necessarily guarantee that you are happy, that you are fairly treated by others, that your problems are solved or that you will always get what you want. One thing **is** certain though: asserting yourself increases your chances of those things occurring.

Part

1

'Action springs not from thought, but from a
readiness for responsibility.'

Dietrich Bonhoeffer

What it means to be assertive

In Part 1 we look at what it means to be assertive and what the alternatives are. You will learn why you might find it difficult to be assertive and what will help to make it easier to be assertive. You will see that changing your behaviour and opting to be assertive in every situation is not the only way forward. Instead, the emphasis is on **choosing** to be assertive – or not.

First you have to learn how to be assertive – then you will be confident that you are making a choice and that you are not just avoiding confrontations because you are afraid. Once you are an assertive person you don't have to be assertive at all times – you can behave in other ways, when it is appropriate and if you are prepared to take responsibility. Part 1 will explain how to do this.

Chapter 1

'It is not the mountain we conquer but ourselves.'

Edmund Hillary

What does it mean to be assertive?

What does it mean to be assertive and what are the alternatives?

'Just shout loudly and carry a big stick', is what one friend replied when I asked him how to be assertive.

But assertiveness isn't about being loud and threatening or always getting your own way. That is aggression. Keeping quiet and going along with what others want isn't always the best way to behave. That is being passive. Manipulating others and avoiding responsibility for getting your needs met is not a fair way to behave either. That is being passive–aggressive.

Assertiveness is an entirely different approach to meeting your needs. It is about letting others know what you do and do not want in a confident and direct way. Both passive and aggressive people relate to others as though only one person counts: themselves. In contrast, assertive people are concerned with a fair deal for everyone.

"Assertiveness is about letting others know what you do and do not want in a confident and direct way."

Although you can think of assertiveness on a continuum between passiveness and aggressiveness, assertiveness includes understanding the boundaries between these different behaviour and communication styles.

- Assertive: being confident and direct when communicating with other people.
- Aggressive: being arrogant, forceful and determined to get your own way.
- Passive: deferring your own needs and wishes in favour of others' needs and wants.
- Passive–aggressive: indirect and manipulative communication and behaviour.

Let's look more closely at each behaviour and communication style.

Assertive

Being assertive is an honest and appropriate expression of your feelings, opinions and needs. When you are assertive you are able to let other people know what you do and do not want. This means calmly stating your needs, what you will or will not accept and how you want to be treated.

You can choose whether or not to tell other people what you think, how you feel and what you believe. You can handle criticism without tears or tantrums. You do not let a fear of conflict silence you and are prepared to take the consequences of communicating your feelings and wants.

Being assertive means you do not feel you have to prove anything, but neither do you think you have to allow yourself to be mistreated. You set boundaries, and feel entitled to defend yourself from exploitation, attack and hostility.

When you are being assertive you are open to other people's views, even though they may be different from your own. You do not try to dominate others or involve yourself in put-downs.

You have the confidence to make decisions and take responsibility for what you say and do. You do not blame other people when things don't go your way. You can give and receive both compliments and criticisms.

You feel that the world is an OK place and you are just as important as everyone else. You know that you have rights and so does everyone else.

Aggressive

Aggressive behaviour and communication also involves expressing your feelings, opinions and needs but in a way that threatens, dismisses or controls other people.

When you are aggressive you may feel you have to prove things and push a point. If you feel you are being treated badly you react with anger and hostility.

Rather than being honest and direct, aggressive communication often involves being rude, sarcastic and blaming.

Aggression is a win–lose situation. You win and others probably lose. It is a one-way process – you say what you do and do not want but do not listen to or take other people's needs and feelings into consideration. If you are aggressive you talk over and interrupt others. Aggression is about domination and invasion; it is fundamentally disrespectful of other people's personal boundaries.

A relationship based on the aggression of one person usually gets worse unless the aggressive person is willing to change or others are willing to be more assertive.

You feel the world is a tough place and you're going to push your way through it.

Passive

Passive behaviour and communication involves not expressing your thoughts, feelings and needs.

Being passive means letting other people dominate you and tell you what to do and not do. You are easily manipulated by others and let their needs overrule yours. You do not say what you do and don't want or what you think. You find it difficult to stand up for what is right or wrong, or how you want to be treated. You often go along with others even when you do not agree with them.

If you are passive you avoid friction of any kind. You may fear the reaction of others so stay quiet and agreeable.

Your agreement is frequently misinterpreted. On the one hand, it leaves others uncertain of your feelings so they ignore or disregard you. On the other hand, it can lead others to take advantage of you. You often find yourself dumped with tasks you did not really want to do.

It's easy for other people to disrespect you. You are often indecisive so let others make the choices and make things happen. It's a win–lose situation. They win, you lose. You don't feel you have any rights – you often blame yourself when things don't go your way.

If someone is nasty or unfair towards you, you will keep feelings of injustice buried inside.

Passive behaviour can result in you feeling disappointed in the relationships you have, and not feel in control of your life.

You feel the world is a difficult and scary place. Other people's needs and opinions are more important than yours.

Passive–aggressive

Passive–aggressive communication is an indirect and dishonest expression of your feelings, opinions and needs. It involves an avoidance pattern of behaviour – avoiding saying what you really do and do not want.

If you are passive–aggressive, you manipulate people to get your own way. You control situations and people without seeming to. Typically, rather than saying what you do not want, you display a passive resistance to meeting the needs and expectations of others.

You procrastinate, find excuses for delays, or 'forget' about what you were asked to do. You may even create a sense of chaos so somebody else will offer to take action instead.

You often suppress your anger and frustration and use a non-verbal way of expressing it – for example, giving others 'the silent treatment' or 'dirty looks' when you are unhappy with them. This does not, though, let others know what you are really feeling.

You may also be in the habit of using sarcasm and other subtle characteristics to avoid confrontation or avoid doing certain tasks.

You are often deliberately obstructive and uncooperative, you will avoid responsibility for doing your share and manipulate others to make the decisions and do things for you.

If you can find a way to blame others then you can shirk the responsibility for your own feelings and emotions that, in fact, you brought about by your own actions. You lose, I lose – both people suffer.

You are adept at devising ways to catch others' attention. For example, you rarely come on time to a meeting or party. You want others to wait for you and give you importance.

You feel the world is an unfair place and you are going to avoid responsibility and blame other people for it.

When is it OK to be aggressive or passive?

If being assertive is the most effective, positive way to behave and communicate, why do we behave in other ineffective, negative ways? It is all down to our fight or flight response. This response evolved in primitive men and women to protect them from animals and humans that threatened their physical survival.

"Why do we behave in other ineffective, negative ways?"

11

	Assertive	Aggressive	Passive	Passive–aggressive
Attitude	I'm OK, you're OK	I'm OK, you're not OK	I'm not OK – you're OK	I'm not OK, so you're not OK
	Flexible, open	Inflexible	Resigned	Negative
	Optimistic	Narrow-minded	Pessimistic	Stubborn
	Confident	Belligerent	Timid	Sulky
	Decisive, positive	Hostile	Self-deprecating	Suspicious, disrespectful
	Aware, warm, kind	Prejudiced	Accepting	Pessimistic
	Supportive, willing	Blaming	Placating	Blaming
	Secure	Uncooperative	Anxious	Easily offended
	Appreciative	Unappreciative	Uptight	Envious
				Resentful
Behaviour	Constructive	Destructive	Submissive	Destructive
	Problem-solving	Self-centred and selfish	Compliant	Manipulative
	Solution-focused	Excluding	Helpless	Self-centred
	Negotiates	Violent	Directionless	Selfish
	Cooperates, listens	Domineering	Disconnected	Blaming
	Interested	Attacking		Underhand
	Inclusive	Insensitive		Sabotaging
	Able to give and take compliments and criticism	Punitive		Intentionally inefficient
				Undermining
				Procrastinating
				'Forgets' obligations
				Avoids responsibility
				Makes excuses and lies

Voice	Calm, steady and even Encouraging Sincere	Loud Forceful Abusive Sneering Sarcastic Critical	Quiet Mumbling Monotonous Waffling	Dismissive Critical Sarcastic Moaning Complaining
Words	Shall we? What do you think? I need I would like Thanks	Stop it Don't Won't Can't Do it NOW Piss off It's your fault You *always* …	Sorry It's not up to me It's only me It doesn't really matter I don't know I don't mind It's up to you	Now what have I done wrong? It's not fair This will never work Can't I haven't done it yet
Body language	Balanced, open gestures Head up Eye contact Smiling	Sharp, angular gestures Space-invading Eyeballing Frowning	Shrinking Hunching Fiddling	Avoiding eye contact Frowning False smiling Fiddling

Fight was expressed by physically confronting the threat, and flight was expressed by retreating.

Nowadays, we still have our fight and flight responses, but rather than fight or run away from stressful situations, we have a wider range of behaviours included in each response. The fight response is exhibited in typical aggressive behaviour: selfish, dominating, angry, loud. The flight response can be observed in passive behaviour such as giving in to other, more dominant people, being timid and quiet, anxious or resigned.

In modern times, we may not meet many dangerous animals or marauding invaders, but when we do face dangers to our physical survival, the fight or flight response is still invaluable.

When activated, the fight or flight response causes a surge of adrenalin and other stress hormones to pump through our body. This surge is the force that allows a person to run through the flames of a burning house to rescue a trapped child, or to stay low and quiet if an intruder is ransacking their house.

More often, though, today's threats are likely to consist of an uncooperative boss, a rude shop assistant, your hostile teenager or critical partner. They are all capable of provoking the same fight or flight response as bears and tigers and enemy marauders. Much as you may want to, you know it is counter-productive to, for example, slap your boss when he or she provokes you. On the other hand, it is also counter-productive to run away from him or her!

There are, however, occasions when it is a positive advantage to be passive or aggressive. Anger is a very powerful and useful emotion. There is nothing wrong in being angry – it is how and when you express it that matters. There is also nothing wrong with keeping quiet and submitting to other people's needs and demands – when it's appropriate and as long as you do not behave this way all the time.

As you can see, there are advantages and disadvantages to each behaviour style, which is why, subconsciously, you may behave and communicate in one way rather than another.

Advantages and disadvantages of aggressive, passive and assertive behaviour

	Assertive	Aggressive	Passive	Passive–aggressive
Advantages	Others have respect for you You are more aware of what you do and don't want Your needs are more likely to be met You take others' needs into consideration	Other people fear you You get attention You get your own way	Other people like you and think you are easy to get on with You don't have to make decisions Other people feel sorry for you You don't have to take responsibility	You can manipulate a situation to get what you want or need You get attention You get your own way You don't take responsibility
Disadvantages	Other people may be jealous or resentful of you Other people may see your persistence and determination as aggressive There's no guarantee that you will or won't get what you want and don't want	Other people fear and avoid you Other people resent and dislike you Other people may retaliate with equal force You may feel guilty or disappointed in yourself	Other people walk all over you You have no control You get left out or used Your needs aren't met	Other people get confused and frustrated by you Other people may resent and dislike you Other people avoid you

15

Unlike people who are unassertive, when an assertive person is aggressive or passive, he or she will take responsibility for choosing to behave or communicate in an aggressive or passive way. For example, if the normally assertive person is being aggressive, he or she will acknowledge it: 'Yes, I'm very angry.' Assertive people defend themselves when someone else attempts to dominate them, using any method necessary, including force. Assertive people use aggression defensively, never offensively.

On the other hand, an assertive person may choose to respond in a passive way and admit, 'I am not going to react or do anything about it. I choose to withdraw.' They may not like being dominated, but they see it as the best option at the time – to avoid the possibility of violence or some form of coercion.

In contrast, an aggressive person will not take responsibility for their actions – they will say that they were provoked. A passive person will say they were made to do something by other people. A passive–aggressive person will use either of those responses.

Why do you struggle to be more assertive?

There are a variety of reasons why you may struggle to be assertive. Most of your ways of behaving and communicating are established when you are very young. Your upbringing, past and current relationships, past losses and disappointments may cause you to feel you are not able to take control of your life.

Gender has an impact too. Our culture tends to accept aggressive behaviour in men and passive behaviour in women. So men who are unable to say what they do and do not want, how they feel and what they believe may express themselves aggressively and women who are reluctant to assert their needs and beliefs express themselves passively.

Let's understand why you might behave in any one particular way.

Aggressive behaviour – why do you do it?

Aggressive behaviour is often the result of being ignored, misunderstood, cheated or put upon, in the short or long term. You might only behave aggressively in particular situations, for instance after drinking alcohol or when you feel that you are being undermined or laughed at, or when you are feeling impatient, angry or very upset.

A pattern of responding in an aggressive way can be learnt behaviour – you may have been brought up to believe that behaving aggressively to get what you want and to refuse what you do not want is normal and acceptable.

Passive behaviour – why do you do it?

If your parents, teachers, siblings or friends were dominant and controlling, then you may have felt invalidated so much as a child that now you are afraid to speak up. If you were taught that others should come first then you may feel that it is not OK for you to ask for what you want. I once heard two small, excited children in the bakery ask their grandmother to buy them each a cake. 'What have I told you?', she asked. 'Those who ask don't get!' What?!

It's understandable that if you've been discouraged from asking for what you want, and are afraid of displeasing others and of not being liked, you will avoid asserting yourself. You may think that others will be hurt, angry or disappointed if you do not do what they want.

You may believe that you do not have the right to state your needs and opinions. Typically, if you find it difficult to make decisions, if you do not know exactly what you want in any one particular situation, you will go along with others who have stronger opinions.

These types of beliefs and behaviours can be deeply ingrained. The theory of learned helplessness suggests that as a result of the negative outcomes of past experiences, passive people have *learned* to become helpless and resigned and perceive (rightly or wrongly) that they have no control over current and future events, so they are unwilling to even try to change things.

Assertive people, on the other hand, have a much more positive outlook: they believe that they can positively affect situations.

This tendency to anticipate the best possible outcome is, of course, optimism. Optimism allows you to feel in control of your life and believe that there is something you can do to manage your feelings and cope.

Even though your beliefs and attitudes may have been learnt, your outlook is not fixed. Your beliefs and attitudes are not permanent – you can learn to think and behave in a more positive, assertive way, as you will see in this book.

"Even though your beliefs and attitudes may have been learnt, your outlook is not fixed."

Passive–aggressive behaviour – why do you do it?

You may express your hostility and resentment towards others in passive ways because you learnt that to express your needs, opinions and feelings was unacceptable, rude or selfish.

If, as you were growing up, any display of anger, frustration or disappointment was discouraged or even punished, you have learnt to find less detectable ways to get your needs met and feelings expressed that would not directly jeopardise your relationships.

If you behave in a passive–aggressive way it may be that you lack the self-confidence to ask for, do or say what you really want. A passive person will simply resign their fate to the decisions of others. In contrast, if you are passive–aggressive you are not at all happy to submit to the whims of others but you are reluctant to assert yourself. So, you allow others to take charge and then you resort to underhand ways, such as manipulation and sabotage, in order to get what you do or do not want.

Certain circumstances may trigger passive–aggressive behaviour: situations where you think your abilities or performance will be judged; any situation where you have to deal with authority figures (parents, your manager, teachers and dominant friends) will often provoke indirectly angry behaviour.

When you behave in a passive–aggressive way, although you know you cannot express your feelings overtly, you probably do not even realise you are behaving so manipulatively.

Why is it difficult to be assertive?

Some of the reasons why you might find it difficult are because:

- the other person is confusing or scaring you;
- the other person may become angry or upset;
- you are not sure of your rights;
- you are indecisive;
- you get no response from the other person;
- you lose control;
- you are feeling tired or stressed;
- you lack confidence or feel insecure; and
- you can't think of any other way to deal with the situation – you don't know how to be assertive.

What reasons might **you** have for being unable to be assertive?

The role of self-esteem and confidence

Your ability to be assertive is very much linked to your self-esteem and confidence. How come?

Suppose you accept that to be assertive you have to be honest and direct about your feelings, opinions and needs. You understand that if you are going to be assertive you need to let other people know what you do and do not want.

Simple, right? No. Why not? Because you need self-esteem and confidence to be assertive.

Confidence is a belief in your ability to do something. You need confidence to say what you do or do not want. You need confidence to tell other people what you think and how you want to be treated. You need to feel confident about your ability to handle the consequences of asserting yourself. You need confidence to make decisions and to take responsibility for what you say and do.

A good level of self-esteem means that you have positive feelings about your self-worth and your abilities.

If you are in the habit of not asserting yourself, you find yourself in a 'catch-22' or double-bind situation where one inaction influences the other inaction. You are trapped by two seemingly contradictory demands.

For example, not telling a friend that you are offended by her remarks because you don't want it to appear that you are over-sensitive not only leaves you feeling frustrated with your friend but bad about yourself for not expressing your feelings. You might even tell yourself that if your friend valued you, she would not talk to you like that. This leads you to doubt yourself and your abilities even more, which lowers your confidence and decreases your chances of asserting yourself.

The result? You bury your hurt feelings and they come out in another way – either you sabotage your friendship with passive–aggressive behaviour or, months later, you drag out every perceived past injustice and provoke a big row.

Do assertive people ever feel anxious about expressing their needs and wishes? Of course they do, but the difference between them and non-assertive people is that they take action and take responsibility for the outcome. Rather than focus on how much fear and anxiety they feel, they deal with other people and situations *despite* their fears or worries. They recognise they have to start somewhere!

The impact of different people and situations

Different people and particular situations can affect your ability to be assertive. If the other person is aggressive, if they undermine your confidence or scare you, if you're worried that you won't be able to cope with their response if they become angry or upset, it can be difficult to assert yourself.

If the other person is passive, if they are negative, anxious, insecure, uptight and disengaged, it can be difficult to be assertive.

If the other person is passive–aggressive, if they are easily offended, confuse you, ignore you or sulk, it can be difficult to be assertive.

If, on the other hand, the other person is assertive, they treat you with respect, support and listen to you and it's far easier to be assertive.

Certainly, other people and certain situations can affect your ability to be assertive. But, often, your expectations of others can be a barrier to assertiveness.

Expectations, values and rights

Ask yourself: do you have reasonable expectations of other people? You may need to adjust them.

Often, we believe that there is a right and wrong way that others ought to behave towards us. We may expect more from a relationship than it can deliver. Then, when others fail to meet our expectations, we feel let down, upset and resentful. Most of the time, we are completely unaware of how our expectations can create all sorts of communication breakdowns, misunderstandings, conflicts and distrust.

If you (consciously or unconsciously) harbour expectations that are too high, you set yourself up to feel disappointed, frustrated and angry with yourself and other people. On the other hand, if your expectations about yourself, about life, or about others are too low, it's difficult to express yourself or to take part in or achieve anything.

You expect your friends, for example, to be loyal, honest and trustworthy. If these expectations are violated, you may be angry or upset. You may then internalise those feelings and behave passively or passive–aggressively. Or you may externalise those feelings and behave in an assertive or aggressive way.

It's possible that if, in your childhood, you did not receive much in the way of affection, guidance and support, you may expect that others will not take your needs into consideration either.

If too much was expected of you, you may also be self-critical. The part of you that is self-critical is the part of childhood that may represent the echo of your parents' and other adults' expectations and demands on you. Often, instead of recognising their expectations and demands as unrealistic, you project onto others the same critical attitude that your parents and teachers used on you.

You may find yourself spending time and energy trying to change others to fit an image of what you think they should provide for you. Having realistic expectations means that you take responsibility for your own life instead of looking to others to meet your needs. Once you become aware of unrealistic expectations, you are in a position to do something to free yourself from being dominated by them.

Even better, once you behave and communicate more assertively, other people are more likely to treat you in the way you expect: with respect!

When is it easier to be assertive?

We have looked at some of the barriers to being assertive. When, then, is it easier to be assertive?

It's easier to be assertive when:

- you feel confident
- you value yourself
- you have realistic expectations
- you have support from other people
- you are informed
- you know what your values are
- others listen to and treat you with respect
- you know you have rights.

Values and rights

"Those are my principles. If you don't like them I have others.**"**

Groucho Marx

It is easier to be assertive when you know what your rights are. For example, if you buy a toaster from a shop and, when you get it home, it does not work, you know that you have a legal right to a refund.

However, personal rights are different from legal rights. Legal rights are determined by the State. Personal rights are decided by ... you. Only you can decide what your personal rights are. Your rights are related to your values – the things in life that are important to you and have some worth to you.

What is important to you? What do you value?

When the things that you do and the way you respond match your values, you feel confident that you are doing and saying the right thing. But when what you say and do does not align with your values, that's when things feel wrong.

This is why making an effort to identify your values is so important.

Life can be much easier when you know what your values are – and when you respond to others and make decisions that correspond with your values.

If you value family life, but your manager regularly expects you to put in a 60-hour week in your job, will you make a stand and refuse? And if you *don't* value competition, and you work in a highly competitive marketing environment, for example, are you likely to feel confident and happy in your job?

In these types of situations, knowing your values can really help. When you know your own values, you can use them to make decisions about situations and decide whether to compromise, negotiate or be firm with your position.

So, take the time to understand the priorities in your life, and you'll be able to determine the best direction for you.

Use the following list of common personal values to help you get started.

Accountability

Accuracy

Belonging

Commitment

Consistency

Compassion

Confidentiality

Dependability

Equality

Generosity

Inclusivity

Independence

Loyalty

Patriotism

Patience

Pride

Punctuality

Reliability

Self-control

Support

Transparency

Truth

You may find that, while some values have little or no significance to you, there are those values that just jump out and you feel, 'Yes, this value is important to me'. This values list is merely a guide to get you started; feel free to add these values.

Do these values represent things you would support, even if your choice isn't popular and it puts you in the minority?

When you consider your values in decision making, you can be sure to keep your sense of integrity and what you know is right, and approach decisions with confidence and clarity. You'll also know that what you're doing is best for the current situation. Making value-based choices may not always be easy. However, making a choice that you know is right for you is a lot less difficult in the long run.

"Your values are a central part of who you are."

Your values are a central part of who you are – and who you want to be.

"If you don't stand for something you'll fall for anything."

Author unknown

Although your values are stable and fixed they are *guiding* principles: they are not set in stone, they will need to be flexible according to different situations. There will be times when you will need to know which value is more important to you.

Write down your top five values. Look at two of those values and ask yourself, 'If I could satisfy only one of these, which would I choose?'.

So, truth might be a value, but if in pursuing it you have to compromise other values – calm, peace or good mental health for example – you may want to reconsider. Be aware that when making a decision, you may have to choose between solutions that may satisfy different values.

Also, throughout life, your values may change. For example, in your teenage years fun, friendship and loyalty might have been top priorities. But years later your values may have shifted; tolerance, self-discipline and reliability may be more relevant and what you value more.

So, be aware of your values but revisit your values every now and again. Especially when you're uncertain of how to respond in a situation.

Your values will inform your rights. For example, if you value privacy, you may feel that it is your right for your personal information not to be made public. If you value loyalty, you may feel that it is your right to expect others to be faithful and trustworthy. And if you value forgiveness, you may feel it is your right to make mistakes. Although you will also believe that these rights extend to other people, values and personal rights are subjective – they are based on your experience and expectations of yourself and others. Someone else's personal rights will be based on their experiences and expectations, so they may well be different to yours.

"Values and personal rights are subjective."

What rights do you feel entitled to?

Identifying your personal rights can help you to be clear about your values and expectations.

Here is a sample of those rights.

You have the right:

> To ask for what you want without feeling guilty.
>
> To ask for information.
>
> To express your thoughts and feelings.
>
> To make your own decisions and cope with the consequences.
>
> To choose whether or not you should be responsible for solving other people's problems.
>
> Not to know about something, or not to understand.
>
> To make mistakes.
>
> To be successful.
>
> To change your mind.
>
> To privacy.
>
> To be alone and independent.
>
> To choose not to be assertive.
>
> To make changes.

What rights would you add to this list? Ask yourself: do the rights you choose for yourself apply equally to other people?

"The basic difference between being assertive and being aggressive is how our words and behaviour affect the rights and well-being of others."

Sharon Anthony Bower

Believe in your rights and the rights of others. Say what you think, feel and believe but also give others their rights too.

When you are assertive you are able to stand up for your rights and behave and express yourself in ways that do not violate another person's rights.

Aggressive behaviour means that because you express your needs and opinions so forcefully, you are violating other people's rights.

Passive behaviour means that because you do not express your needs, thoughts and feelings, you do not assert your rights, which then opens the door for others to violate your rights.

Passive–aggressive behaviour means that because you are under-hand and manipulative, not only are you not expressing your rights, but you are also violating other people's rights. You both lose out.

Assertive behaviour is based on a philosophy that we all have personal rights, which enable each of us to take assertive action.

The importance of assertiveness in all areas of your life

You have it in you to be assertive at all times, but, as we have already seen, certain people or situations can have an impact on your ability to be assertive or not.

Perhaps you find it easy to say 'no' to your friends, but find it difficult to refuse requests from colleagues at work. Maybe you have no problem telling a friend how annoyed you are that she always turns up late, but cannot cope with your sister phoning to cry on your shoulder (again).

If you are assertive in some areas, but not others, the chances are this is linked to where your insecurities lie. Do you find it hard to decline extra work from your boss? Maybe you are worried about job security. Possibly you feel confident about your job security but find it difficult to be assertive with your teenage daughter. You don't want to insist she helps with chores around the house because you're worried she'll leave home to move back in with her father.

If you are not confident about carrying out a task and feel your actions are being judged, you may find it difficult to assert yourself when challenged about what you are doing, but if you are skilled at what you do you will have less of a problem coping with someone who challenges your actions or motivations.

Top tips

- Assertiveness involves letting others know what you do and do not want in a confident and direct way. It also means being open to the views and opinions of others, even though they may be different from your own.

- There are advantages and disadvantages to being passive or aggressive. It's OK to be angry – it is how and when you express it that matters. There is also nothing wrong with being passive – when it's appropriate and as long as you do not behave this way all the time.

- When an assertive person is aggressive or passive, he or she will take responsibility for choosing to behave or communicate in that way. Unassertive people often blame others for 'making' them behave in that way.

- There are a number of reasons why you may find it hard to be assertive. They include your upbringing, your beliefs and expectations, relationships, disappointments and levels of confidence. Other people's behaviour will also have an impact on your ability to be assertive.

- The way you behave and communicate, your beliefs and attitudes do not have to be fixed – you can learn to think and behave in a more positive, assertive way.

- Identifying your personal rights can help you to be clear about your values and expectations.

- Believe in your rights and the rights of others. Say what you believe, do and do not want but also give others their rights too.

Quiz

How assertive are you? It's not always easy to know. In some situations and with some people you may feel quite capable of being assertive. But in other circumstances you may find it difficult to express yourself honestly and clearly. The quiz that follows will help you to recognise your levels of assertiveness and work out in which situations and with which people you could be more assertive.

In the left-hand column is a variety of situations and assertive responses. In the right-hand column you rate each situation with marks out of ten. You may, for example, find saying 'no' to a friend when she asks you to babysit difficult to do, so you would rate it with a 2. On the other hand, if a colleague appears to be avoiding you, you may not have a problem asking her if she is upset or angry with you. You would probably rate that situation with a 9 or 10.

How assertive are you?

Use the following questions to see in which areas of your life you feel least and most assertive. In each section: over 50 = excellent; over 30 = not bad; under 30 = this area needs attention. As you read the book you will find suggestions about how you could respond.

Assertiveness in the workplace	Mark out of 10 (where 10 is easy; 1 is impossible)
Your boss accuses you of being lazy. You stand up for yourself calmly and confidently.	
You are asked to give a presentation to a committee. You look forward to it.	
Your colleague hasn't done his share of a mutual project. You criticise him without getting angry.	
You feel that you have been producing some really good work. You prepare your case and ask for a pay rise.	

Assertiveness in the workplace *continued*	Mark out of 10 (where 10 is easy; 1 is impossible)
A colleague at work is bad-tempered and snaps at you. It doesn't bother you and you just ignore it.	
You already feel overworked but your manager has asked you to take on more work. You tell her you won't be able to do this.	

Assertiveness with friends	Mark out of 10 (where 10 is easy; 1 is impossible)
You tell a friend that you are annoyed that he doesn't pay his fair share when you are out together.	
In a group of mutual acquaintances, a good friend who isn't there is the subject of malicious gossip. You speak up for your friend.	
A friend asks you to babysit on a night when you already have other plans. You ask for time to think about it and then say 'no'.	
A couple of friends have told you that you have made comments about them that they have found offensive. You thought they were funny but apologise and admit they were right.	
A friend says that she admires the way that you tell stories and can make everyone laugh. You enjoy the compliment and say 'thank you'.	
You go to a restaurant with a group of friends. You skim-read the menu and you are the first to decide what you want.	

Assertiveness with your family	Mark out of 10 (where 10 is easy; 1 is impossible)
Your brother-in-law criticises your newly-decorated room. You use humour and laugh at his comments.	
You praise your teenage children for unpacking the shopping and clearing the table.	
Your mother telephones every day and expects you to visit. You tell her that you will not be able to visit as often in future.	
Your father tells you that you deal with the children well and that you are a good parent. You accept the compliment with pleasure.	
You tell your partner that you are not happy about his lack of commitment and his frequent absences from home.	
You sit down with your family and discuss with them a list of jobs that you would like them to do in future.	

Assertiveness with service providers	Mark out of 10 (where 10 is easy; 1 is impossible)
You are sitting alone in a busy restaurant and the waiter ignores you. You go over to him and ask him to serve you.	
The doctor diagnoses your health problem and says what can (and cannot) be done about it. You get confused and do not understand. You ask her to repeat her explanation and give you time to write it down.	
The sales assistant has gone to a lot of trouble to find a selection of shoes for you but none of them is exactly the style you want. You leave without buying anything.	

You buy new flooring to be fitted in your living room. The flooring isn't fitted on the agreed date and later develops a fault. You clearly explain what you want done about it.	
In a restaurant children are running around, shouting loudly and banging into tables. You ask the manager to speak to the parents about their children's behaviour.	
You are attending a course. A couple of the other students continually disrupt the class. You talk privately to the tutor and ask him to intervene and manage the situation.	

Assertiveness in interviews	Mark out of 10 (where 10 is easy; 1 is impossible)
You have been invited to attend an interview at a large local organisation. You research the company by carefully reading their website.	
You are waiting in reception and the interviewer arrives. You stand up, smile, look the interviewer in the eye and put forward your hand to shake.	
You are asked a question that you do not understand. You say you do not understand the question and ask the interviewer to please repeat it.	
You are asked about your skills and strengths. You describe what they are and give examples.	
You are asked about your weaknesses. You give examples and either say what you are doing to work on your weaknesses, or explain how your weaknesses can also be seen as strengths.	
The interviewer makes a dismissive remark about the last place you worked at, saying that it is a second-rate company. You disagree and explain why.	

What the scores mean

Total your score for each separate area (family, friends, etc.).

Over 50: no one gets one over on you, do they? You probably have little difficulty asserting yourself in this area!

Over 30: not bad, but you need to improve your assertiveness levels in the specific situations where you had a low score.

Under 30: you have probably scored poorly in most situations in that area and need to concentrate on the guidance given in the book.

Now that you have read Chapter 1, you will realise why you find it difficult to be assertive in certain areas of your life. Read the rest of Part 1 to understand the theory of how to become an assertive person. However, we realise that understanding the theory and putting it into practice are very different. To help you, in Part 2 we look at specific situations from the quiz and examine how best to handle them assertively. Your scores will show you in which parts of your life you are least assertive, but it is probably best to start with the areas that you find the easiest. Look at the suggestions and try them out in real life – it's the only way to learn!

Chapter

2

'Everyone thinks of changing the world, but no one thinks of changing himself.'

Leo Tolstoy

Feel good about yourself and make others feel good too

Making changes

If you have read the last chapter, you will have understood that there are a number of differences between assertive, aggressive, passive and passive–aggressive behaviour. You will also have understood that there are a number of reasons why you might behave assertively in some situations and unassertively in others.

You will have realised that there are areas in your life where you could improve your assertiveness and you will have accepted that you have strengths and weaknesses.

Ready to make some changes? Not sure? Not to worry.

The prospect of changing the way you behave and communicate can be quite daunting. If you are feeling apprehensive, you may be tempted to keep to your usual habits and patterns of behaviour.

Rather than hide from your concerns and remain stuck in your old ways, you are more likely to change your behaviour if you acknowledge your worries.

> "You are more likely to change your behaviour if you acknowledge your worries."

Worries may include the fact that change can bring:

- uncertainty
- disruption

- instability
- confusion
- risk
- loss.

Changing the way you behave in the world is a risky business, and the results are not guaranteed. But focusing on the negative aspects of change can paralyse you and stop you from moving forward.

> ### Exercise
>
> Of course it's going to feel strange, behaving differently. But you can adjust. If you want to prove that to yourself, try the following experiment. Select any object you have around you most of the time – let's suppose you've chosen a clock. Now move the clock to another part of the room. How often do you glance in the wrong direction when you want to check the time? Confusing, isn't it? But if you stick with it, after only a couple of weeks you will have adjusted to behaving in a new, different way.

If you really are motivated to make a change, you will be more likely to focus on the *positive* aspects. And, if you focus on the positive aspects of change, you will be more inclined to make those changes! Positive aspects of changing the way you communicate and behave include:

- improved relationships
- improved self-esteem and confidence
- greater influence and control
- a sense of achievement
- new opportunities.

A word of caution: rushing headlong into new ways of coping and communicating with other people is rarely the best means of ensuring that it becomes a permanent way of behaving. Preparation is crucial.

Research[1] has shown that there are seven stages involved in a change in behaviour. This process is the same for any behaviour change – whether it is, for example, quitting smoking, taking up running or being assertive.

Seven stages of change

Pre-awareness stage

In this first stage, you are not even aware that you need to or can make any changes. It may be that someone else has issues with your behaviour but that doesn't mean that you agree. If you don't think a problem exists, you won't be motivated to make any changes.

Identification and contemplation stage

This involves recognition of the need to make a change. Your decision to consider behaving differently may be an emotional response and/or it could involve rational, conscious thought.

Maybe someone else has a problem with your behaviour or you want things to be different. You are aware that there may be some benefits of changing, but are not confident about your ability to change.

Preparation stage

This can be a protracted stage and may involve several different steps, such as:

- looking for signs and evidence that you should make changes
- weighing up the pros and cons
- looking for ideas and information about how to behave differently
- deciding whether the time is right
- understanding what you need to do
- formulating specific, positive goals.

In the preparation stage, you intend to make some changes but, first, you may be thinking about and looking for signs to confirm that you really do, in fact, need to change your behaviour. You may feel that certain criteria need to be in place before you can make changes.

Biases can creep into your decision to change or not change your behaviour. You will probably be willing to accept facts that support conclusions you've already reached about your behaviour but disregard other facts that support different conclusions.

For example, your mother might not like the way you behave but your brother says that Mum is the problem, not you, so you happily conclude that you don't need to change. You then terminate any further search for evidence that you do need to change!

What else can influence your decision to move to the next stage of change and take action? If you understand what you need to do and if you can foresee a possible outcome, you are more likely to take action. If you feel that making a change is in accordance with your needs, abilities and values, you are more likely to alter your behaviour.

Timing is also very important; you might feel, for example, that because jobs in your department aren't secure at the moment, now is not the right time to start being more assertive at work.

In this preparation stage you will need to identify precisely what behaviours you want to address (the quiz in Chapter 1 will have helped you to do this) and you will need to establish your objectives – that is, you will need to clearly define your goals.

"You will need to identify precisely what behaviours you want to address."

Recognising, for example, that you want to be less aggressive and more assertive is commendable, but you will need to be more specific. So, instead, one of your goals might be to stop raising your voice every time you want someone to do something for you. Conversely, if you want to raise your assertiveness levels, a more clearly defined goal could be to stop mumbling when you want to request a favour.

Positive goal setting

A helpful thing to know here is that thinking, for example, 'I have to stop mumbling when I need a favour' or 'I must stop yelling when the children misbehave' doesn't tell you what to do instead of mumbling or yelling. Thinking, 'When I want to ask a favour I'll speak clearly and make eye contact' or 'When I feel angry, I'm going to take deep breaths and speak calmly' will give you a positive goal. If you want to eliminate an unhelpful behaviour, you must also decide what positive behaviour to substitute.

Any behaviour change has a greater chance of success when you define it in positive terms instead of negative ones. Too many intentions to change focus on negative goals – to quit, to stop or to lose.

If you set yourself a negative goal, such as 'to stop being so critical', then your mind will focus on the negative words 'stop' and 'critical'. Resolutions that contain 'don't', 'mustn't' or 'stop' are self-defeating. Instead of thinking, 'I must stop being so critical', think, 'I am going to be more tolerant and accepting'.

You are more likely to achieve goals that get you what you want, rather than goals that get you to avoid something! Your preparations for change should inspire you and give you hope. Positive goals do this. In contrast, negative goals that are framed in terms of 'mustn't', 'can't' or 'won't' create doom and gloom and don't serve to motivate you.

Behaviour you want to change	What you want to do instead	How you feel about the prospect
Criticising the clothes my son wears	Focus on something he wears that I do like	Looking forward to the challenge!
Agreeing with my colleague to work late	Tell him I intend to finish on time every day	Anxious but determined to finish on time

Worried it's going to take too long to achieve your goals?

'If I start becoming more assertive with my teenage children now, it could take months to see a real change in their behaviour.'

Thinking like this can paralyse you. If you don't take action, those months will pass anyway and nothing will have changed!

Resolve to make a positive change in your behaviour and then ask yourself, 'How does working on this aspect of my behaviour make me feel right now?'. Does it inspire you, bring some hope and give you a focus? It does? Then start working towards it!

Of course, your goals are in the future, but in reality you are only ever in the present. Thinking about and setting positive goals will improve how you feel right now.

However, if a goal doesn't improve your current state of mind, then why have it? If you feel that it is going to create too much sacrifice and anxiety, if you are worried about the risks you will face and other discouraging thoughts, then it is not a realistic goal. Drop it and consider another aspect to develop.

Action stage

This is the stage where you actually put the changes into place. You modify your behaviour or change one way of behaving for another.

The action stage is typically stressful and requires time and energy, but with good preparation it can also be an exciting time that results in new ways of behaving and communicating.

Depending on the goals and plans you made in the **preparation** stage, the action stage can occur in small, gradual steps, or it can be a complete life change.

Maintenance stage

Here, you will be working to keep up your new ways of communicating and behaving. You will want to avoid old habits and patterns of behaviour and you may well be looking for ways to avoid being tempted to revert back to unassertive behaviour.

Termination stage

By this stage you will have established new ways of behaving. You will permanently have adopted more effective ways of communication and behaviour. You will have recognised that former problem behaviours are no longer an option. (For example, you know that you are not prepared to leave a meeting feeling angry and frustrated any more just because you didn't have the courage to voice your disagreement.)

Any change in communication or behaviour should involve you moving from one stage to the next. Each stage is preparation for the next one, so hurrying through or skipping a stage is not going to be as effective as progressing from one stage to the next.

Progress, change and relapse stage

In any change of behaviour there is a possibility that you will make mistakes and lapse back into your usual way of behaving and communicating. Relapse is normal and to be expected. If you do relapse, you might experience feelings of failure, disappointment and frustration. The key to success is to not let these setbacks undermine your determination and confidence. It is crucial that you realise this – do not let a relapse make you give up!

If you lapse back into your old way of interacting with others, try and identify why it happened. What triggered the relapse? What can you do to avoid these triggers in the future?

Maybe you were trying to bite off more than you could chew, or your goals were too generalised? For example, deciding that 'I want to be nicer to everyone' is too big an ask! Instead, 'I am not going to snap at my colleague every time she says something I don't agree with' is far more achievable.

You might want to reassess your motivation, techniques and commitment to your goals. Also, make plans for how you will deal with any future setbacks. By approaching a goal with an understanding of how to best prepare, act and maintain a new behaviour, you will be more likely to succeed.

If you do relapse back to your old ways of behaving and communicating, it is unlikely that you will fall back completely to where you began.

Typically, you will take two steps forward and one step backward – making progress and losing ground, learning from mistakes and using what you have learnt to move forward.

It is even possible that you will go through the cycle a number of times before the new way of interacting becomes established.

Adopting any new behaviour takes practice, so be patient with yourself. Since old habits don't vanish overnight, you are likely to have a few relapses.

"Since old habits don't vanish overnight, you are likely to have a few relapses."

Don't think of difficulties as failure; it's far more conducive to think of slip-ups as integral to the process – opportunities to learn, do better next time and slowly build your confidence.

Prepare for change; feel good about yourself

As well as not letting setbacks undermine your confidence and determination to change your behaviour, you will feel more confident about being assertive if you identify the skills and strengths that will support you in your efforts to become more assertive.

Strengths are a combination of behaviour, skills and knowledge that you apply consistently to produce a successful result.

Everyone can identify a handful of strengths that are very much their own, but how do you know if each one is a strength?

It's a strength if:

- it feels real – 'this is the real me';
- by using that strength, you are able to do things easily and quickly;
- you often want to act in accordance with that strength; and
- you feel positive rather than negative when you use that strength.

The strengths we're interested in here are those that are relevant to assertiveness.

If, for example, one of your strengths is that you are a good listener – then you already have one of the building blocks to assertiveness. Why? Because being a good listener means that you already find it easy to acknowledge other people's needs and feelings.

Below is a list of strengths that are related to assertive communication and behaviour. Tick each one that applies to you. Think about all different areas of your life where you might demonstrate these strengths – work, family, friends and leisure.

Accountable	Dutiful	Open-minded
Achiever	Empathic	Optimistic
Adaptable	Encouraging	Organised
Affectionate	Enquiring	Patient
Altruistic	Enthusiastic	Peaceful
Appreciative	Fair	Persistent
Approachable	Flexible	Punctual
Calm	Forgiving	Reassuring
Caring	Generous	Reliable
Committed	Helpful	Respectful
Compassionate	Honest	Responsible
Conscientious	Hopeful	Risk-taker
Consistent	Impulsive	Sincere
Cooperative	Inclusive	Spiritual
Curious	Independent	Spontaneous
Decisive	Just	Sympathetic
Dependable	Kind	Tolerant
Determined	Loyal	Willing
Diplomatic	Modest	
Discreet	Observant	

Now, choose your top three strengths. When have you used those strengths? In what ways and in which situations?

When you remember times you have drawn on those strengths that are related to being assertive, you will undoubtedly start to feel more confident about being assertive.

If, for example, your strengths include being determined and persistent, you may recall a time when you stood your ground when someone tried to railroad you. If you are kind and caring, you will probably remember times when you were concerned for and able to take others' points of view. And, if one of your strengths is your ability to take responsibility, you will know that you find it easy to be accountable for your actions and decisions.

The importance of positive people

As well as identifying your personal strengths, it will also help you if you identify the positive people in your life. These are the people who you can be yourself with, who value your opinion and who make you feel good. In fact, in many ways, they will be the people you know who are assertive – people who will tell you what they think and are open-minded about the views and opinions of others.

Positive people

Who are the positive people in your life? Different people have different attributes. One might be the friend who motivates and inspires you, while someone else might always be the right person to celebrate your successes and cheer you up when times are tough. The person who you can turn to for advice doesn't have to be a close friend; he or she could be a good therapist, someone in a support group, a colleague or your hairdresser. Be creative in thinking about who are the positive people in your life. Whoever they are, they can be a real source of strength, inspiration and support in your move to be more assertive.

You may already be familiar with the concept of other people being radiators or drains. Radiators spread warmth and positivity and make you feel confident and inspired; however, drains sap your energy and discourage you – their negativity can leave you feeling irritated and depressed.

How to spot a drain? Their behaviour includes being critical and sarcastic, moaning and complaining. 'Drains' can be needy and self-centred. Typical passive–aggressive behaviour!

Often, the advice is to reduce the amount of time you spend around drains. Certainly, that is an option, but here we are concerned with assertively dealing with the drains!

How to feel good about yourself and step into the virtuous circle!

Once you have identified your skills, strengths and the positive people in your life, you can take action from a position of strength.

In Chapter 1 we established that your ability to be assertive is very much linked to your self-esteem and confidence. Confidence is a belief in your ability to do something. You need confidence to say what you do or do not want and you need to feel confident about your ability to handle the consequences of asserting yourself. However, if you are not in the habit of asserting yourself, you find yourself in a double-bind situation – unable to assert yourself because you don't have the confidence, and unable to feel confident because you rarely assert yourself. You are trapped by two seemingly contradictory demands!

The good news is that it works the other way round, too! It **can** be a win–win situation. If you assert yourself you will feel more confident the next time; your new-found, higher level of confidence will motivate you to assert yourself. Remember – confidence is the ability to take action, however difficult and scary it might feel at the time.

> "Confidence is the ability to take action, however difficult and scary it might feel at the time."

One way forward is to take small steps that will build up your confidence. Do not, for example, risk being shot down by an outpouring of wrath from your domineering mother-in-law or your boss because you want to say you do not agree with her about how she thinks a task should be done. Instead, aim to start by being assertive with a more amenable friend – someone who is more likely to cooperate when you assert yourself.

Manage those feelings – take control and take action

Do assertive people ever feel anxious about expressing their needs and wishes? Of course they do, but the difference between them and non-assertive people is that they take action and take responsibility for the outcome. They do not let fear of the outcome paralyse them.

Acknowledge and accept how you feel

When you are assertive, the focus is not on how much fear and anxiety you feel, the focus is on dealing with other people and situations *despite* your fears or worries. You recognise you have to start somewhere!

For example, imagine your sister-in-law often puts you down. You don't have the confidence to defend yourself because you fear the consequences. What if the family starts to take sides and your husband becomes upset that family harmony has been disrupted?

However, imagine you grabbed the cow by the horns and calmly confronted her. Imagine that despite being concerned about consequences, you told your sister-in-law how you felt about her comments.

You might want to leave it at that, but you might then have found the confidence to add that you weren't going to stand for it any longer. That if, in future, she makes remarks like that you will invite her to explain and clarify what, exactly, she means and that you may refute or disagree with her put-downs but you will not stay quiet any more. And there's more. Imagine you had already thought it through and pre-empted the consequences – you told her that you knew other family members might not like it that you were rocking the boat but you would deal with that.

The result? You have:

- confronted both your fears and your sister-in-law
- said how you feel

- set boundaries
- exercised your right to defend yourself from hostility
- made it clear that you would take responsibility for the consequences.

That's one hell of an achievement!

Accepting your weaknesses

If you have completed the quiz, you will have identified the people with whom and situations where you could be more assertive. Like everyone else, you will have both strengths and weaknesses – it's simply a part of being human. Accept that and you've made a good start!

A realistic, albeit subjective, appraisal and acceptance of your weaknesses does not mean that you have to resign yourself to them, it simply means accepting that **past** behaviour, attitudes and beliefs **cannot** be changed.

Assertive people don't dwell on their weaknesses, instead they learn from their mistakes and experiences: they recognise what they might have done differently and resolve to do it differently next time. Assertive people know that **future** behaviour, attitudes and beliefs **can** be changed. What happens next, what happens in the future, is open to change. This sort of positive attitude puts you in control!

Speaking fluent body language

Your body language plays a big part in being assertive. Even if you are silent you are still communicating – through your posture, facial expressions and appearance.

You use your body to help you communicate and to emphasise what you want to say in words. Interestingly, when communication is difficult our body language becomes more pronounced. It doesn't take you long to notice that someone is angry if they are using big, short, sharp gestures. You can also tell that someone is anxious if they are fiddling and twiddling!

Poor eye contact, slouching, nervous gestures and other unassertive behaviours can reinforce negative communication. On the other hand, a balanced posture and calm voice and gestures can help communicate an assertive approach.

Physical movements can reveal many things about the person using them. Non-verbal behaviours communicate who you are and how you feel. Other people draw conclusions from your body language about your sincerity, credibility and emotions.

Being more aware of and regulating your body language can make all the difference to your ability to assert yourself appropriately.

Posture

Your posture is often influenced by your emotions, which means if you are feeling angry or frustrated you may jut forward your shoulders, jaw and chin.

Placing your hands on your hips establishes authority, or communicates that there are 'issues'.

If you are feeling intimidated or anxious, you may slouch, drop your chin and hunch your shoulders forward. This gives away that you are not feeling comfortable and chances are that others may feel just as uncomfortable in your presence.

To show confidence and assertiveness, simply stand straight and keep your head level. Relax your shoulders and spread your weight evenly on both legs.

Even when you are feeling intimidated, if you can master the self-assured posture you will immediately start feeling more confident. You can affect your mood or emotions simply by changing your posture.

Try out your confident posture in front of the mirror and make yourself aware of what your confident stature looks and feels like.

Distance

Learn what the most comfortable personal space distance is for you. Allow yourself enough room to feel at ease and move when necessary.

Gestures

Do you fiddle with your hair? Bite your nails? Fidget with jewellery? Then even if you are not feeling tense or nervous, you will still come across as though you are.

Do you use hand and arm gestures in nearly every sentence? Try to avoid a continuous physical interpretation of everything you say. Instead, add gestures selectively where they provide the most impact. If you convey your feelings with words and a facial expression, your arms can relax to your sides because they aren't needed.

Eyes

Have you ever been talking with someone who did not look at you directly? The person looked over your shoulder, at the floor, or even at someone else – everywhere but at you. It is most likely that you felt uneasy or frustrated and you doubted the other person's interest. Do not try to talk to someone who has their back to you, who is texting, reading, on the computer or watching TV. Instead, wait until you have their full attention. Look directly at the other person when you are being assertive but avoid eyeballing or allowing yourself to be eyeballed.

Voice

Rather than say how you feel, do you purse your lips if you are not pleased about something? Be careful – other people are not easily fooled!

If you mumble or whine, you are not coming across as assertive. Instead, you are conveying nervousness and tension (even though that might not be how you are feeling). The same impression is given if you use 'filler' words such as 'actually', 'like' or 'you know'.

Try to speak slowly, audibly and calmly. Avoid gabbling – rapid and indistinct words confuse people and can result in your not being understood or taken seriously.

How is your handshake?

A handshake says a lot about you and what you communicate. Does your handshake lack confidence and oomph? No one wants to shake a hand that is as soft as a wet noodle. On the other hand (get it?!) a handshake needn't be a contest of strength. It's a handshake, not arm wrestling.

How to shake like you mean it? Practise. Simply practise with a friend till you both agree you've got it right and you can shake with the best of them!

Appearance

Like it or not, how you dress does affect your credibility. The clothes you wear, the colours and styles all say something about you.

You've probably experienced an occasion when you were over-dressed or underdressed in relation to others. At the very least it can leave you feeling uncomfortable and, at worse, it can completely drain your confidence. Feeling good about your appearance can help to encourage an assertive approach.

Wearing clothes that reflect your personality and make you feel comfortable and confident does not need a lot of money or time, just a belief that you deserve to look your best.

So, head up, speak up, smile and shake hands. You too can learn to become more assertive by speaking fluent body language!

Giving and receiving compliments

A further, effective way of feeling good and making others feel good is through giving and receiving positive recognition. Positive recognition can be expressed as admiration, praise, appreciation or gratitude.

Giving genuine compliments brings you out of yourself, because you have to be more aware of those around you. In order to compliment someone you have to actively look for positive traits or attributes and specific examples.

By doing this on a regular basis (try once a day) people's positive traits start to jump out at you; the more observant you are of those around you, the easier it is to make compliments about them.

Your thought processes shift to looking for the best in people and this proactive approach spills over into other areas of your life. Compliment-giving is a jump-start to identifying all sorts of positive aspects of your life.

"This proactive approach spills over into other areas of your life."

How to give a compliment

Be specific. Sometimes the most memorable compliments are the most specific ones, because it shows that you were paying attention.

The specifics can follow a general compliment or be given alone. For example:

'You look great! I really like the way you've styled your hair.'

'The report you wrote was very good. You made the issues so easy to understand.'

Change the compliment around to reflect the positive effect that the person has had on you. For example:

'Your concern has helped me feel better. Thanks.'

'After listening to you speak, I felt inspired to do things differently. Thank you.'

'That was generous of you – you made my day. Thanks.'

'Your calm approach has reassured me. Thank you.'

When you tell the other person that they have made a difference, he or she can then feel good about themselves (the purpose of a compliment) and encouraged because of the impact their actions had on you. And, there is no way they can deny your compliment without sounding silly: 'No it didn't!'.

A sincere compliment is always a welcome boost to someone's day, although there will be those that reject one. Be aware that for some people, and in some cultures, it is polite to deny compliments and impolite to accept them. Failure to do this is seen as strange or rude. Sometimes, someone may refuse a compliment for this reason.

A compliment is like a gift; if someone doesn't want your gift, you'll still end up owning it. The best way to accept one is also like a gift: just say 'thank you'. In order to accept graciously, all it takes is two words – thank you. Don't say anything negative. If you want to add something, make sure it is positive:

- 'How nice, thank you.'
- 'That's the best thing anyone has said to me today (this week/ in a long time). Thanks!'
- 'Thank you for telling me.'
- 'Thank you. I really appreciate hearing that.'
- 'Thank you. I'm pleased with what I did, too.'

If you receive a compliment on a job well done and you didn't do it alone, make sure to give credit to those who helped: 'Harry and Tom were such a big help. I couldn't have done it without them.'

Remember to accept the compliment without feeling like you have to pay them back. This will make you feel more confident and let you grow to like yourself better.

Top tips

- Focus on the positive aspects of changing your ways of behaving and communicating.
- Identify clear, specific changes that you want to make.
- Changing your behaviour and communication takes time so be prepared for relapses. Remember: two steps forward, one step back.

- Identify your skills and strengths. Identify the positive people in your life. They will support you in your efforts to become more assertive.

- Have courage: deal with other people and situations *despite* your fears or worries.

- Speak fluent body language – it plays a big part in being assertive.

- Give and receive compliments. Compliment-giving is a jump-start to identifying a wide range of positive aspects in your life.

Note

[1] DiClemente, C.C. and Prochaska, J.O. (1982), 'Self change and therapy change of smoking behavior: A comparison of processes of change in cessation and maintenance', *Addictive Behavior* pp. 133–42.

Chapter

3

'Be who you are and say what you feel because those who mind don't matter and those who matter don't mind.'

Dr Seuss

Say what you want and what you don't want

Anxiety, guilt, anger or fear of change; whatever the barriers, one of the main reasons you might find it difficult to say what you do and don't want is that you just don't know how.

Telling other people what you do and don't want includes:

- identifying how you feel
- being clear and direct
- listening and being open to other people's views
- accepting other people's rights
- identifying what the alternative ways forward might be
- asserting your rights and setting boundaries and limits; what you will and will not accept
- knowing when to compromise and negotiate and when to stand your ground and insist
- being prepared to find solutions
- being prepared to take the consequences of communicating your feelings and wants
- taking responsibility and not blaming other people for the outcome.

Identifying how you feel

"People can refute your facts, but never your feelings."

Sharon Anthony Bower

The first step to managing a situation in an assertive way is to notice how you feel.

Asking someone to do something for you, confronting someone about their behaviour, saying 'no' when you want to say 'no' – these kinds of situations all have feelings attached to them.

Try noticing how you *feel* about the situation. Frustrated and angry? Hurt? Anxious, disappointed or jealous? Your feelings and emotions do not define you; they are simply internal messages to yourself that can help you understand your motivations and actions.

"Your feelings and emotions do not define you."

Once you become more aware of your emotions and feelings, you can choose whether to share them. This doesn't mean 'dumping' your feelings on others. But if you do choose to let them know how you feel, you start by saying 'I feel' and not 'You are making me feel'. For example, saying 'You are making me angry' blames the other person for how you feel. On the other hand, saying 'I am feeling angry' is taking responsibility for feeling that way.

Own your feelings

You have a right to your feelings. Rephrasing your feelings and owning them is a powerful way of discovering that it's OK to feel the way you do.

How would you rephrase the last four sentences below?

You're making me angry	I feel angry
You've been dishonest	I feel deceived
You've really upset me	I feel . . . . . .
You've lied to me	I feel . . . . . .
You've been rude to me	I feel . . . . . .
You've ignored me	I feel . . . . . .

Acknowledging how you feel and think about a particular situation can help you be more assertive. How? By helping you to be clear about what you do or don't want. Imagine that your friend asked you to look after her three children at the weekend. Your immediate response? Dread. But instead of saying 'no', you say: 'Yes, sure. I'll have them on Saturday.'

Your feelings of dread are telling you that you want to say 'no'. But instead, you ignore your feelings and agree to look after her children. Uh?

No one is suggesting that you actually say to your friend: 'I dread looking after your children.' The point is, rather than letting your feelings overwhelm you and take over the situation, being aware of how you feel can help you stay in control and inform your response. Listen to and acknowledge your feelings.

Being clear and direct

Having reflected on how you feel, the next step is to identify what exactly it is that you do or don't want, and to be direct about saying it.

What do you want?

What do you think each person does or doesn't want?

Lou: 'I get angry so often because every time I ask you to help with housework you say you've got homework to do. It always gets left to me.'

Theo: 'Who's been smoking? Someone open a window. Ugh, the smell makes me feel sick. Go outside. I thought you were going to give up.'

Ali: 'Er, I bought this DVD from this market stall last week but it doesn't seem to be working properly. I'm not sure what's wrong with it. My children were really disappointed – they were looking forward to watching it.'

Sarah: 'The thing is, I'm not sure what time I'm finishing work tomorrow and, sorry, what film did you say it was? Oh, well, I'm not really into romantic comedies but I did like Jennifer Aniston when she was in Friends. I'll be too tired for drinks afterwards; will the film be finishing late?'

What does Lou want?

    (a) Help with the housework.

    (b) For her son not to have so much homework.

    (c) For her son not to use homework as an excuse.

What does Theo want?

    (a) For a window to be opened.

    (b) For the other person to give up smoking.

    (c) Both of the above.

What does Ali want?

    (a) Her money back.

    (b) A replacement DVD.

    (c) For the stallholder to decide what to do.

What is it that Sarah does not want?

    (a) To see the film.

    (b) To see that film.

    (c) To stay out late.

Not entirely sure what they all want? That's because neither Lou, Theo, Ali or Sarah are clear what they want, either.

You can make it easier for other people to do what you ask if you can tell them clearly what exactly it is that you want.

'Being direct' is a straightforward technique. When you want something, or want to refuse something, get straight to the point. For example:

Lou: 'I'd like you to do the washing up.'

Theo: 'Please would you smoke in the garden?'

Ali: 'I want a refund please.'

Sarah: 'Thanks, but I don't want to see that film.'

Being clear and direct has a number of benefits, including:

- time saving
- other people don't have to second-guess what you really mean
- misunderstandings are avoided
- enabling negotiation to take place
- you are more likely to achieve a win–win solution.

How often, when you do or don't want something, do you use all sorts of indirect ways to let others know? When you use techniques such as hints, excuses, sarcasm or anger, the meaning of what you really want to say is hidden. The only way to ensure that someone has understood what you want is to be clear and direct in what you say.

Take your time

What if you are not sure about how you feel or what you want? Say so. Simply say that you are not sure how you feel about something and need time to think about it.

In American films and TV, you often hear one character say to another: 'Can I get back to you on that?'.

Of course, you might not find it easy to say so, but the aim here is to learn to identify your feelings and needs. There is nothing wrong with saying: 'I'm not sure. Can I get back to you?'. If the other person needs an answer now (and, to be fair, they may have a good reason for needing an immediate response) calmly suggest they will need to ask someone else.

"The aim is to learn to identify your feelings and needs."

Another reason for asking for time out, or a break, is if the conversation becomes too heated. Explain that it has nothing to do with the other person, it is just that you feel confused, tired or need time to reflect and can you resume the conversation later?

Active listening

Once you have said what you do or do not want, you must make a conscious effort to listen to the other person's response. Too often, you might find yourself responding emotionally to what someone said; your expectations and assumptions can distort what you think the other person has said. So it's important that before you reply, you clarify what you think you heard the other person say.

You do not have to agree with what the other person said, just be sure that you have understood. You can check whether or not you have understood the other person by summarising your understanding of what was said and asking for verification. This not only lets you know whether you have understood the other correctly, it lets the other person know they have been understood.

When Jamie responds to his mother's request to do the washing up with 'Not right now, I've got homework', there's very little for Lou to clarify. However, the response that Theo receives is not so clear. Careful listening and verifying are crucial:

Theo: 'I'd like you to smoke in the garden.'

Evie: 'Will you please stop nagging. Honestly, I'm fed up with you going on and on about it. It's not easy to give up, you know.'

Theo: 'OK, I'm not sure what you're saying here. I'm not asking you to give up, simply to smoke outside. Are you saying you won't go out to the garden to smoke?'

By changing your attitude and approach, you may find that others respond differently to you because they sense your ability to listen and understand.

Get more information

It takes concentration and determination to be an active listener. As well as verifying what the other person has said, you may need to ask for more information:

Lou: 'When does your homework have to be handed in?'

Jamie: 'End of the week.'

Lou: 'Fine. Then please wash up now and do your homework another time.'

If, on the other hand, you are the one who is being asked to do something, make sure you understand exactly what is being asked of you before you respond. Perhaps, for example, you are being asked to do something that is more time-consuming than you thought. However, it may not take much effort at all.

Accept other people's rights: compromise or negotiate

Saying what you do and do not want, and acknowledging the other person's response, does not, however, guarantee you will get what you want or need. The other person has a right not to cooperate.

If, when the other person refuses to do what you ask, your usual response is to back down, argue or sulk – stop! Instead, acknowledge the other person's perspective and try to negotiate or compromise with him or her. For example:

Lou: 'I'd like you to do the washing up.'

Jamie: 'Not right now, I'm doing my homework.'

Lou: 'When does your homework have to be handed in?'

Jamie: 'End of the week.'

Lou: 'The end of the week? Then please wash up now and do your homework another time.'

Jamie: 'No. I'm seeing my friends tonight. I want to get the homework done before I go out.'

Lou might claim that her son does not have homework – that he is using it as an excuse to get out of helping out. Maybe he genuinely does have homework that has to be done right now. Either way, Lou should take his right to refuse into consideration.

Lou: 'OK. I'd like the washing up done before you go out with your friends tonight.'

Remember, being assertive does not mean you will always get your own way. When you get a response, you must be prepared for it not being the response you wanted! For example:

Ali: 'I want a refund.'

Stallholder: 'Sorry, but it wasn't me on the stall yesterday and anyway we don't give refunds.'

Sarah: 'Thanks for inviting me but I'm too tired to watch a film.'

Liz: 'That's not fair. I never get to go out. The children are with their Dad tonight and I want to do something.'

Remember that your goal is to behave assertively – to respect both yourself and the other person equally. Do not make changing the other person one of your goals. The other person may or may not change; that is not within your control.

If, like Lou, your request for the washing up to be done is met with, 'No, I'm doing my homework', instead of replying: 'Oh all right, I'll have to do it then' or 'For God's sake, I'm sick of you using homework as an excuse to get out of doing the chores', stop yourself! One way forward is to ask the other person what alternatives he or she might have:

Lou: 'Well, what would be a good time for you to do it?'

This type of response will not only position you as reasonable, it may also lead to a better conclusion for both of you. By changing your attitude and approach, you may find that others respond differently to you because they sense your willingness to be reasonable.

"By changing your attitude and approach, you may find that others respond differently to you."

Negotiate

Fortunately there's a way to say 'no' and 'yes' at the same time: refuse the request, but offer an alternative that works for you and benefits the other person as well:

Lou: 'OK – I'll do the washing up tonight, but I want you to do it tomorrow.'

Sarah: 'Sure, I'll come to the cinema but I won't be going for a drink afterwards.'

Know your limits, set boundaries, stand your ground

If you choose to negotiate or compromise with the other person, bend as far as you can but no further. Once you reach your limit, stop before you create a new set of problems that could take even longer to resolve.

Setting limits is a crucial part of being assertive; your limits define how you allow others to treat you. They should represent the least and the most that you will accept, based on your values and rights. Your boundaries and limits support you in respecting and taking care of yourself.

If you are unclear about your limits, or you have established weak boundaries, you invite others to take advantage of you and take control of your choices. On the other hand, recognising and accepting that you *do* have choices is the first step to consciously setting positive boundaries.

Identifying and maintaining your limits will empower you to choose what to do and not do, in every situation. You will choose to say 'yes' to those things that you want to do or be part of, and say 'no' to those things and people that drain your energy. The choice is yours.

There will be times when you want to stand your ground and refuse to give in. You will not be prepared to negotiate or compromise but will insist on asserting your rights and maintaining your limits.

Accept the response but stand your ground

Calmly respond to the other person in a way that will both acknowledge you have understood what they've said but also confirm you are standing firm:

Lou: *'You may have homework to do*, but I still need the washing up done now.'

Ali: *'Maybe no one else has had a problem*, but I still want a refund.'

Theo: *'It might be cold out there*, but I don't want you to smoke in the house.'

Sarah: *'I know you are disappointed*, but I am too tired to go to the cinema tonight.'

Certainly others might see you as being stubborn, or even think you are being manipulative. But when you assertively set limits, you take responsibility for the outcome. You are prepared to take the consequences.

Setting limits

When Rosa Parks refused to get up from a seat reserved for white people on a bus in Alabama in 1955 she was arrested and fined.

In an interview many years later, Rosa explained that although she didn't plan the incident, when it happened, she decided to stand up for her rights and take responsibility for the outcome:

Were you scared to do such a brave thing?

No, actually I had no fear at that particular time. I was very determined to let it be known how it felt to be treated in that manner – discriminated against. I was thinking mostly about how inconvenienced I was – stopping me from going home and doing my work – something I had not expected. When I did realize, I faced it, and it was quite a challenge to be arrested. I did not really know what would happen. I didn't feel especially frightened. I felt more annoyed than frightened.

Did you know that you were going to jail if you didn't give up your seat?

Well, I knew I was going to jail when the driver said he was going to have me arrested. I didn't feel good about going to jail, but I was willing to go to let it be known that under this type of segregation, black people had endured too much for too long.

How did you feel when you were asked to give up your seat?

I didn't feel very good about being told to stand up and not have a seat. I felt I had a right to stay where I was. That was why I told the driver I was not going to stand. I believed that he would arrest me. I did it because I wanted this particular driver to know that we were being treated unfairly as individuals and as a people.

What were your feelings when you were able to sit in the front of the bus for the first time?

I was glad that the type of treatment – legally enforced segregation – on the buses was over ... had come to an end. It was something rather special. However, when I knew the boycott was over, and that we didn't have to be mistreated on the bus anymore, that was a much better feeling than I had when we were being mistreated.

http://teacher.scholastic.com/ROSA/interview.htm

Of course, it is not likely that you will face arrest when you stand up for yourself. But Rosa Parks's story does go to show that positive change can happen when you set limits and take responsibility for the outcome.

Consequences and solutions

Your limits and boundaries can also help you decide what you will do if the other person does not cooperate with you. This does not mean issuing threats or warnings about punishments. Threats increase the emotional temperature and make an argument more likely. It means coming up with a solution – a specific answer to the problem. This means that you are the one in control because you have decided what you will do if the other person does not cooperate.

For example, Lou told Jamie that if he did not to do the washing up before he went out she would not give him a lift to the party. Sarah decided that the solution to her friend Liz's persistence about going to the cinema would be to tell Liz that she was feeling hassled and would Liz please stop going on about it.

Solutions and consequences differ from a threat or punishment. A threat is a warning that something unpleasant will happen. A punishment is 'getting back' at someone, to hurt them for something you feel they 'did' to you. A solution is a specific answer to a situation. A consequence is a logical result. Solutions and consequences follow naturally from the other person's action or inaction.

When, for example, you get a parking fine, it's not a punishment for something you did wrong. It is a solution (for the local council) to the town's parking problems and it is a consequence (for you) of your poor choices and decisions.

When Lou gave her son a consequence, it flowed naturally from his choice and inaction. Rather than take his phone for a week (punitive and illogical), the solution was not to give him a lift to the party. And to spend the time saved doing the washing up herself.

Take time to think of solutions and consequences, rather than give a knee-jerk reaction, even if this means telling the other person that you are going to take time to think about your response.

The most important question you need to ask yourself is: 'What do I want to accomplish here? A punishment or a solution?'.

Take responsibility for the outcome: do not blame the other person

There may be any number of possible outcomes that could occur if you stand your ground and maintain your limits. Maybe the other person will cooperate, maybe they won't – they might feel resentful, they might sulk, get angry or burst into tears. They may stop talking to you or tell everyone what an awful person you are. You might be pleasantly surprised or you might not. If you stand your ground, you must accept that there will be consequences.

> **"If you stand your ground, you must accept that there will be consequences."**

How often, when you don't get what you want, do you blame the other person? 'He's so unreasonable.' 'It's his fault.' 'She made me do it.' Stop! Stop blaming the other person when you don't get what you want.

In no way does blaming the other person give you control over the outcome of a situation. In fact, it does completely the opposite – it means that you relinquish control – the other person has probably had the last word or the deciding action.

That's fine if you are happy to let go of the outcome, but if you try to blame other people or external factors for things not working out the way you want, you are wasting time and energy that could be better spent on a more positive outcome.

When you rationalise and accept that you are responsible for every response and every decision you make, you are in the fortunate position of knowing that it is you and only you who can determine the outcome.

When, for example, Ali realised that she was not going to get a replacement DVD or a refund, rather than stand her ground she chose to walk away empty-handed. Ali did not blame the stallholder for being uncooperative; she simply decided she didn't want to get stressed about it. 'I actually felt like I was the one in control because I chose to cut my losses and avoid getting angry. I let it go.'

You might think that where you choose to withdraw from a situation, you are being weak and powerless, or that you will lose the respect of others. On the contrary – as long as you accept responsibility for walking away, you are demonstrating your self-worth, level of security and courage.

Once you accept responsibility for your reactions to others, you will soon discover that you are able to find solutions to life's difficulties far more quickly.

The consequences of not taking responsibility for your responses

When you fail to accept responsibility for your responses, either you risk becoming critical and intolerant of others or you risk seeing yourself as a victim of other people's actions.

Thinking that the other person is to blame suggests that you are blameless – they have done something wrong and you have done nothing wrong. This attitude leads to an exaggerated sense of self. Because your perception of your needs and feelings is exaggerated, your expectation of other people is unrealistic and you become impatient, intolerant and demanding. With this attitude, you will find it even more difficult to gain their cooperation. Your relationships will suffer and, before long, very few people will want to be around you.

If, on the other hand, you are more inclined to behave passively, by not taking responsibility for your response (or rather, lack of response) you probably see yourself as a victim – at the mercy of other people's whims and needs.

Stop and think back to the last time you accepted responsibility for something. Does it seem as if you have a difficult time doing it? Once this habit of accepting responsibility and dealing with the consequences is maintained, your ability to be assertive and decisive slowly develops.

Don't feel guilty

You may be responsible for your reactions but you are not responsible for other people's needs. Failing to stand your ground, failing to negotiate or agreeing to do something that you don't want to do are all signs that you could be a people pleaser. People pleasers tend to take responsibilities that aren't theirs; they cannot draw the line without feeling guilty.

If, instead of saying 'no', you feel obliged to say 'yes' to someone's request, you create a new set of problems that could take even longer to resolve!

For example, although she wanted to say 'no', Sarah agreed to go to the cinema with her friend Liz. Instead of taking responsibility for saying 'yes', she privately blamed her friend for 'making' her go out. Sarah deliberately turned up late and, as they were leaving, she muttered that the film had been 'rubbish'. The row that followed could have been avoided if Sarah had simply said 'no' to going out in the first place!

When you say 'yes' to something, you are saying 'no' to something else. In Sarah's case, she was saying 'no' to her own voice telling her how tired she was. Saying 'yes' might seem the easiest or most expedient thing to do at the time, but you may regret it afterwards.

Be aware of what you 'let yourself' be responsible for. If, for example, you choose to meet someone else's needs out of sympathy or compassion then your boundaries are not invaded and feelings of anger, frustration or resentment should not come into play. On the other hand, submitting to the other person just to avoid feelings of guilt is not an honest basis or motive for doing something.

It might be helpful to understand what 'guilt' means. Guilt represents a feeling that you've done wrong. You need to ask yourself: if you assert your rights and do not comply with the other person – what have you done wrong? Let them down? If you feel you are responsible for others' well-being then it's no wonder that you feel guilty. In your mind, you are letting them down!

Once you accept that you are NOT responsible for meeting their every need, you stop being a people pleaser and you stop feeling guilty about saying 'no'.

Certainly, learning to stand your ground, to trust your instincts and respectfully to disagree with others is a difficult thing. Learning how to say 'no' without feeling guilty takes practice and courage. But saying 'no' when you don't want to do something will keep you out of a lot of trouble in the long run.

Get in touch with your 'I'm not happy about this' feelings. If you think you are going to resent agreeing to something, you need to be honest and compromise, negotiate or simply say 'no' to others. It's not their responsibility to protect your boundaries – it's yours.

Saying 'no' without excessive excuses and apologies

" 'No' is a complete sentence.**"**

Annie Lamott

By all means start with 'I'm sorry but … ' or 'I'm afraid that … ', but only apologise once. The other person might have a problem (for example, no one to go to the cinema with) but remember, you do not have to allow her to give it to you. A simple 'I'm sorry, I'm too tired' will do.

As well as only needing to apologise once, you only need one genuine reason for saying 'no'. 'I can't come to the cinema tonight – I'm too tired', rather than, 'I would come to the cinema, but I'm too tired. I have a report to finish and I'm not feeling that well. Also, I'm not sure if my partner will be home in time to be with the children.' If you give too many excuses, the meaning and value of your response starts to look weak and dishonest. It also gives the other person the opportunity to undermine your excuses. For example: 'Not to worry – I'll pick you up and drop off my teenager at your house – he can babysit. I can probably help you finish that report and, anyway, a good film will make you feel much better.' Try getting out of that!

All you need is one valid reason why you do or do not want to do something. Remember – acknowledge the other person's situation, but stand your ground: 'I know you are disappointed, but I am too tired to go to the cinema tonight.' Judge the success of your interactions with others by how well you have behaved. Even if the other person does not change, you can walk away knowing that you have behaved in accord with the principles of assertiveness.

However, remember that assertiveness techniques take time to learn and nobody gets it right all the time. When you fail to communicate assertively, the best response is to apologise. This, at least, leaves the door open for better communication the next time.

In a nutshell

How to say what you want

- identify how you feel and what, exactly, you want
- say what it is that you want
- listen to and acknowledge the other person's response
- stand your ground and stick to what you want

or

- compromise and negotiate

How to say what you do not want

- notice how you feel
- say 'no'
- listen to and acknowledge the other person's response
- stand your ground and insist

or

- compromise and negotiate

Top tips

- Identify and own your feelings. Say 'I feel' and not '**you** are making me feel'.

- Be clear and direct about what, exactly, it is that you do or do not want. Assert your rights; set boundaries and limits and know when to stand your ground. Identifying and maintaining your limits will enable you to choose what to do and not do, in every situation.

- Listen and be open to other people's views and rights. Resist the urge to back down, argue or sulk. Instead, acknowledge the other person's perspective and try to negotiate or compromise with him or her. Aim for solutions and alternative courses of action.

- Be prepared to take the consequences of communicating your feelings and wants. Do not blame other people for the outcome.

- Don't feel guilty and don't make lots of excuses or apologies for communicating what you do and do not want.

Chapter

'Don't mind criticism. If it is untrue, disregard it;
if unfair, keep from irritation; if it is ignorant, smile;
if it is justified it is not criticism, learn from it.'

Mark Twain

How to deal with other people's expectations and demands

Let's imagine that you work in an office and one morning you receive this message:

'Mr Barnes would like to see you in his office at 2pm. Sharp.'

Assuming that Mr Barnes is your superior – how would you react?

Was your immediate response to think, 'I wonder what I have done wrong?'

Or perhaps, 'I wonder if he's going to offer me the promotion I've been after.'

Or, 'This will be interesting. I'm looking forward to hearing what he has to say.'

We've tried this out with the classes that we teach and, almost without fail, people say that they would immediately assume that they had done something wrong. One woman said she felt sick just hearing that sentence.

The next thing to imagine is how you would spend the next three hours before you went to see Mr Barnes. Would you find it difficult to concentrate on your work while your mind went into overdrive remembering all your recent shortcomings and failings? Would you begin gathering together your 'excuses' in readiness (a recent bereavement, illness, moving house or splitting up from a partner)? Would you mention it to other people at work and ask them if they had any idea what it could be about or what kind of mood he was in? Would it ruin your lunch hour and either put you off your food or cause you to eat lots of 'comfort' food and sweet things?

If any (or all) of the above describes your likely behaviour in this kind of situation then you are not alone. Receiving criticism is the one aspect of assertive behaviour that almost everyone seems to find difficult. Notice that in the example it is the dread of criticism that has caused you such anxiety – you haven't even heard what he has to say yet.

"It is the dread of criticism that has caused you such anxiety."

Why do I react like this?

If you look back at your life, you can probably remember times when you have been criticised. Children are routinely criticised on a daily basis. At home, they are told off for being mean to their siblings, not doing what they have been asked to do, breaking things, being dirty, not eating their food, not eating their food nicely, not sharing their toys – in fact any, and every, aspect of behaviour and appearance.

At school, you may remember comments on your work: 'This really isn't good enough' or, perhaps even worse, 'You could do better than this' (when you had worked hard). Many people can remember an occasion when they were told off or criticised at school (particularly if it was unjust). Some teachers seem to think that sarcasm is a way of maintaining order in their class (only if they are the ones giving the sarcastic comments, of course). Schoolchildren often tell me how difficult it is to be assertive with adults as any polite defence they try to make is greeted with, 'And don't you dare answer back'.

Did you dread your school report and savour any praise in those short, ubiquitous phrases? Were you anxious on parents' evening about what the teachers might say about the standard of your work and your behaviour in class? Did your parents berate you and repeat the criticisms they had received, and add to them, when they got you alone?

Add to this the likely possibility that you were bullied at some stage in your childhood and it is not difficult to see why adults react badly to criticism. Some children grow impervious to criticism and know that behaving badly is a fail-safe way of gaining attention. But most children want to please, and try desperately to gain the approval of those they respect.

Were you bullied as a child?

About 80% of bullying takes the form of name-calling, ridiculing, fault-finding and verbally abusing the victim (whereas physical bullying is comparatively rare – even in schools). In schools, verbal bullying reaches its peak at the start of secondary school and is usually delivered by the same-sex, same-age children. We now also have electronic bullying – unpleasant text messages, emails, instant messaging – which means that bullying can now invade what was previously the sanctuary of the home.

If you were bullied as a child, the chances are that you don't like to talk about it, even now. There is something about being bullied that makes children feel ashamed; they feel guilty as though it is their fault. They are reluctant to tell anyone because they feel hopeless – there is nothing anyone can do – and if they tell it will only get worse.

Mean and aggressive behaviour is confusing to children, and adults, who come from families where the assumption is that people behave in a civil way towards each other. If your family has always dealt with problems by talking in a calm and rational way it can be bewildering to deal with people whose sole aim seems to be to cause misery and suffering with their cruel comments.

There is a tendency for people who are being bullied to think that the person taunting them must have a valid reason for doing so and that if they can just change, or improve themselves, then the comments will stop. Many anorexics can trace their issues with food to comments about their size; adults who opt for cosmetic surgery often admit that it is because of criticism about their nose or breasts; other people dye their hair or get contact lenses because of painful school memories of being called 'four-eyes' or 'ginger-nut'.

If you did experience bullying as a child, it may have made a lasting impression on your self-esteem. You may have been getting on with your life and managed to submerge the past, when along comes someone who somehow seems to say things deliberately to upset you and you are reduced to that child crying in the playground.

Bullying in the workplace

"One in four people are bullied at work and 18.9 million working days are lost each year as a result.**"**

www.andreaadamstrust.org

Bullying in the workplace, or even at home, is very similar to the bullying carried out by schoolchildren. The difference for adults is that the shame and the guilt may be even greater – causing the victim to remain silent and to feel inadequate, hopeless and sometimes even suicidal.

In the workplace, bullying can take the form of intimidation – setting unrealistic deadlines – so that you feel that you must stay late or take work home in order to survive. Being closely scrutinised all the time is another form of insidious pressure, as well as having your work constantly criticised in front of others.

Cary Cooper, Professor of Organisational Psychology and Health, Lancaster University, studied a sample of 5,500 people who were bullied at work. Writing in *The Independent* (23 February 2010), Professor Cooper said: 'Whatever form bullying takes, it damages an individual's self-esteem, self-confidence, their health and their ability to perform effectively in the workplace. We should not, as a society, tolerate this behaviour.'

For a bully to be able to thrive at work, or at school, there must be an environment that accepts aggressive behaviour, perhaps in the form of competitiveness, along with inadequate training and non-existent, or ignored, codes of conduct.

The person who is being bullied often fails to name the behaviour as such and simply thinks that they are not good enough and that they must work harder, or change, in order to please. Just as the schoolchild thinks that being bullied is their fault, so many adults put up with being humiliated as though they somehow deserve the abuse.

Bullying at home

Similarly, a bullying personality will thrive in a dysfunctional family. In adult relationships, the counselling organisation Relate classifies bullying as domestic violence and says one in four women suffer from it.

If there is a marked difference in the balance of power (either financial or status), someone with bullying tendencies will take advantage of it. Typical tactics are making derogatory comments in front of other people – *'Don't bother asking her, she wouldn't understand'*. Some bullies simply withdraw affection. Living with someone who sulks for days on end can be as soul-destroying as physical abuse.

Just as in the workplace, for the bully to succeed there must be an acceptance of their behaviour. To tolerate bullying means that you are giving a message that it's fine to treat you in that way – that you deserve no better. Again, staying silent and telling no one reinforces their power and your sense of isolation. This is what enables the bullying to continue. A bully could not operate in a healthy relationship where there is respect for each other and support from other people.

What makes a bully?

Although some children go through a bullying stage and then grow out of it, others may learn that aggressive behaviour is a way of getting what they want. Of course, a bully isn't someone who bullies constantly – much of the time they can be smart and good fun to be with. One of the reasons why teachers at school fail to recognise bullying going on under their noses is because bullies can be very clever and charming people.

People seem to think that bullies can see into their inner soul and know exactly what their Achilles' heel is – not realising that bullies just use their superior skill to see what merits a reaction. If you nod and laugh, they try something else – their ability to sense a reaction would be commendable in other circumstances. As soon as you blush, or your eyes fill with tears, or you react in any way other than a casual shrug, then they know they have got you. It's not magic – just a clever use of finely tuned emotional skills.

The reasons people bully are a combination of personality and experience. As a teacher I was always fascinated by the psyche of the bully, and once I could get them to open up and be honest they often admitted to being bullied at home – by older siblings or sometimes a parent. Some bullies simply lack empathy: they have failed to mature in this way and have never learned to be sociable or aware of other people's feelings. Others have simply learned that it's an effective way to get what they want.

Children who are lacking in self-confidence are often desperate to belong and so they attach themselves to the bully – because they are afraid of becoming victims themselves. They become bullies by default. Those who are prepared to put their own moral scruples aside in this way are also much more likely to be vulnerable to peer pressure in other areas such as cigarettes, alcohol and drugs.

Sometimes people bully by example: if a man has seen his father bully his mother – and get away with it – then that is his 'husband' role model. If a teacher has experienced teachers who were sarcastic and ridiculed them, then that is their model. If your mother always shouted at you and constantly put you down you may find yourself controlling your children in the same way.

Adults can bring their bullying behaviour with them to the workplace. If they have never been confronted, or understood the misery of their victim, then they see it as normal, justifiable behaviour that gets results. Some managers just have no idea how to deal with people because they have had no experience or training. Often the reason for adult bullying is work overload – they cannot cope – and aggressive behaviour intimidates people into doing what they want.

The difference between bullying and criticism

It is useful to understand and recognise the difference between bullying and criticism so that you know how to respond. Criticism is the judgement of the merits and faults of someone's work or character. For someone to be able to judge you in this way implies that they have a personal relationship with you or that they have some kind of expertise in this field. Valid criticism can be between parent and child, friend to friend, spouse to spouse, teacher to student, or manager to colleague.

The word 'criticise' implies an expression of disapproval; typically the intention, when someone criticises you, is to point out a fault, shortcoming or weakness (usually in behaviour or appearance). Sometimes people criticise just to be cruel, or because of their own insecurities, but it doesn't make them a bully unless they do it continually. The purpose of constructive criticism is to be helpful so that you can do something about it and, if you agree, improve.

The intention with bullying, however, is always to hurt and humiliate you. The bully is not trying to point out your faults so that you can do something about them – they are intimidating you to make themselves feel superior. There is absolutely no point at all in trying to please or pacify the bully as this will only give them more power, which they will use to make you feel worse.

For adults, the most common kinds of bullying are deliberate, hurtful and persistent comments. So if someone makes a one-off unkind remark we wouldn't call it bullying – it has to occur over a period of time. Casual remarks can still be insensitive and upsetting of course: if someone says, 'When's the baby due?' – thinking you are pregnant when you are not – it would be distressing but that would not have been their intention. It is not deliberate or persistent – so wouldn't be defined as bullying.

People who have been bullied in the past will nearly always react badly to criticism because they have never forgotten the hurt and the shame. As soon as they are in a situation where they are likely to receive criticism they will find themselves feeling either angry and hostile or sick and close to tears.

In the past, bullying was the victim's shameful secret; the good news is that bullying is now out in the open. All schools and most workplaces have bullying policies and there is a National Bullying Helpline (see Appendix 2 for a list of useful organisations and their websites). This means that if a person thinks they are being bullied they have the right to complain and to expect that some action will be taken (this includes everyone, even the Prime Minister).

"The good news is that bullying is now out in the open."

Back to Mr Barnes

'Mr Barnes would like to see you in his office at 2pm. Sharp.'

So, you have been summoned to Mr Barnes's office and have somehow got through the last three hours.

He asks you to sit down and you try to look relaxed and to smile at him. You notice one of your reports on his computer screen. He stands up and begins to pace around the room.

'How long have you been with us?'

'Er, three years.'

'And how many times have I had to speak to you about your work and timekeeping?'

'Once or twice.'

'I think it is a lot more than that. It's simply not good enough. You are often late and your work is careless. What do you have to say for yourself?'

So what would your reaction be? What would you say? Would you be able to answer calmly and assertively or would you feel angry? Perhaps you would feel like bursting into tears, offering up excuses and running from the room? Let's look at the alternatives:

a. The aggressive response

'How dare you speak to me like that? There's nothing wrong with that report – it took me hours! Anyway, if you weren't always giving me things to do at the last minute then maybe I would have had time to redraft it.'

b. Indirect aggression

'Well, I'm sorry Mr Barnes. I don't know what I can have been thinking.' (That is positively the last time I am ever staying late to do any work for him. He can get his own tea in future and I'm never making excuses for him again when he's out of the office.)

c. Passive

'I'm so sorry, Mr Barnes. I'll do it again straightaway and I promise I'll never make any mistakes ever again. I'll come in early from now on and I'll work late tonight to get it done.'

d. Assertive

'Can you tell me exactly what I have done wrong?'

'Look at all these errors.'

'I can see that there are some literals – is there anything else? Would you like me to redo it?'

Reacting to criticism

It is natural to feel defensive when you are being criticised. We have looked at some of the reasons why you might already be sensitive to criticism, but the fact is that most people don't take it very well. The anxiety and defensiveness that we feel when we think we are going to be criticised causes us to overreact; we experience the criticism as a rejection – just as we did as a child.

Can you think of any label that you were given as a child? Were you the 'clumsy one'? Or the 'selfish one'? Or the 'lazy one'? These labels are often perceived by children as describing not only who they are but as disapproval, or a withdrawal of affection and love. By the time we are adults, certain words and phrases can cause us to feel full of self-doubt and uncertainty.

The fear of criticism stops people from saying what they want to say, doing what they want to do, living how they want to live and being how they want to be. Adults (and children) become over-anxious and eager to please in order not to receive negative comments. Parents give in to their children's demands in order not to seem mean; workers stay later and later at the office to forestall any hint of criticism about their attitude; teenagers copy the actions of their friends to stop any sense of disapproval.

a. The aggressive response

The aggressive response to criticism is to refuse to listen. You are either very sure of yourself and believe that you could not possibly have made a mistake, or you are very scared and this is an automatic, habitual reaction.

The next step for an aggressive person is immediately to deny the criticism, followed by a hostile attack on the critic. (*'Anyway if you weren't always giving me things to do at the last minute ... '*)

The consequence? This would almost certainly develop into a row – a shouting match producing a lot of bad feeling. Probably you have avoided being asked to do the work again, but your future prospects could be affected. People who react in this way often take their mood away with them, and no doubt their work colleagues, friends and family would also suffer the brunt of their antagonism.

b. The indirect aggressive response

Indirect aggression is often not recognised by either person. You are furious at the criticism but smile and appear to take it well; inside you are seething and plotting revenge. (*'That's positively the last time I'm ever staying late for him ... '*)

The consequence? This kind of reaction appears to satisfy both parties. Ultimately, however, it can have the effect of making you feel bad about yourself. It is hypocritical to feel an emotion and then to behave in an entirely different way. Taking revenge can be sweet for a moment but it can have lasting repercussions and mean that you develop a reputation as someone not to be trusted.

The way to feel good about yourself is to be authentic. Behave in an honest way that you believe in and that makes you feel proud of yourself.

c. The passive response

Passive people accept criticism without question. They tend to believe that if someone says something about them then it must be true. They feel self-pity: 'It's not my fault. No one understands what my life is like'; or guilt: 'I know that I'm lazy and that I don't work hard enough'; or loss of self-confidence: 'I'm just hopeless. I shouldn't be doing this job – I'm obviously not clever enough.'

The consequence? Passive people rarely stick up for themselves because they are afraid of conflict and people not liking them. However, what often happens is that their very passivity is annoying. They make unrealistic promises, *'I'll do it again straight-away and I promise I'll never make any mistakes ever again'*, in order to fend off further criticism.

Passive people can bring out the worst in some people because they allow their bullying tendencies free rein. It is actually quite difficult to have a relationship with a passive person because you constantly have to check that something is what they really want.

A common phrase is 'No, you choose. I don't mind.' This can be extremely irritating and cause the kind of reaction that the passive person was trying to avoid in the first place. In the work-place it may suit the boss to have a lot of passive people, but in the end it is not a recipe for good working practice and effective relationships.

d. The assertive response

Assertive people listen to the criticism, ask for more information – *'Can you tell me exactly what I have done wrong?'* – then decide whether the criticism is valid or not: *'I can see that there are some literals.'*

It takes courage to be assertive: it means inviting specific criti-cism and perhaps being prepared to admit that it is true. But you won't die – they won't shoot you – so what is there really to be afraid of?

You are an adult – develop an adult ego. This means that you can listen to what other people say about you without reacting in a childish or inappropriate manner. It means that you are fully aware of your right to be treated with respect and to say 'I don't know' or 'I made a mistake', without thinking that it means you are hopeless or a dreadful person.

Here's how to face the music

1. Make sure that you are in a good state of mind. Don't go round telling everyone and working yourself up into a state before you even get there. If possible, go outside for a walk or get some fresh air.

2. Remind yourself of all the times you have been praised recently. (It's a good idea to save emails and notes, however casual, which thank you or pay tribute to something you have done; they might come in useful – but mainly they make you feel good about yourself. Write down compliments people have given you – at the time. Create a folder for them on your computer.)

3. Take the initiative: remember your body language. Walk into the room confidently, look Mr Barnes in the eye and shake his hand (if appropriate). Thank him for sparing the time to talk to you/giving you the opportunity to talk to him.

4. If the criticism is too general, ask for more information; asking for examples is always a good idea if you genuinely don't know what someone is talking about. This is *negative enquiry*: actively encouraging criticism in order to use it (if helpful) or exhaust it (if manipulative).

5. React honestly: 'I feel a bit shocked by what you have said. It has given me a lot to think about.'

6. If you need it, ask for time to think about it: 'Do you mind if I get back to you on this one?' (But make sure you *do* think about it – there's no point asking for more time if you then block it out of your mind and avoid him, hoping he'll forget about it.)

The next step

Decide whether the criticism is valid – or not

Learning to be assertive means examining how you usually react to criticism. Most people find that their initial reaction is to be defensive; once you recognise this you can stop yourself from doing it. As long as you continue to respond defensively to criticism you will continue to get upset and to find relationships, with certain people, very difficult.

Relax and allow yourself to listen to what the other person is actually saying. Paraphrase the criticism so that you both know that there is no misunderstanding. Breathe deeply and stay calm.

Once you have put this into practice and managed to stop immediately defending your actions you will be able to consider whether the criticism is justifiable. If you still don't know, consider whether this has ever been mentioned to you before. You might also consider the qualifications of the critic – do they understand the situation?

If valid

If the criticism is valid:

1. Accept it firmly and confidently: 'Yes, I have been late recently.' This is *negative assertion*: accepting your errors and faults by agreeing strongly and sympathetically with criticism about your negative qualities. It can be quite disarming to the critic.

   (BUT make sure that you're not being self-deprecating: 'I know I talk too much', said in a timid manner, is different to, 'I do tend to talk a lot – particularly when I'm anxious', spoken in a confident, but honest, way.)

"Accepting your errors and faults can be quite disarming to the critic."

2. Decide what you are going to do about it: 'I'm making an effort to improve my timekeeping.'

   (If you are not prepared to change, say so – but accept the consequences. Don't apologise if you secretly like this aspect of your character: 'Yes, I am untidy. I think it is creative.')

3. If you agree with the criticism, but can't think how to change it, ask for help: 'That's true. Can you suggest any way that I can improve?'

4. Thank the other person for constructive criticism: 'Thank you for taking the time to discuss this with me.'

5. Once they've calmed down and heard what you have said, now is the time to state your defence *briefly*: 'Sometimes, I feel that I'm not given sufficient time to write a report.' Don't whine and play the victim – '*poor me*' – just say what you think in a confident manner. Do not go into long, self-critical rationalisations or excuses.

(It may be helpful to preface your defence with, 'I feel nervous saying this to you but … '. However, only use this with people you know and trust – not people pushing in front of you in a queue, or your nasty neighbour.)

If not valid

1. Reject the criticism firmly and confidently: 'No, that's simply not true.' (You can *always* say this if the criticism is too general – 'You're lazy, mean, hopeless, etc.' – as this is just a put-down.)

2. Respond with 'I' statements rather than 'you' statements: 'I think there has been a misunderstanding', rather than, 'You've got it all wrong.'

3. If you are feeling intimidated by criticism, say 'Could you say that again/I don't understand'. This is useful as it makes them have to start all over again – usually more calmly.

4. If the criticism is partly true, agree with the criticism but qualify it: 'I have been late occasionally to meetings but I'm never late for work.' You could try: 'I think that's unfair.'

5. If your critic is speaking quickly and loudly, keep your voice low and speak slowly. Once again it is your body language and tone of voice that is all-important here; make sure that you are not so stung by the unfair criticism that you respond aggressively.

6. Sometimes, when you are baffled by the criticism that you have received, try to rephrase it and see if it actually applies to the critic. So, if someone says, 'You're very money conscious' (and it's untrue), consider whether you've ever thought that they were a bit mean. You could accuse them of hypocrisy if you wanted to get into an argument about this, but otherwise just say, 'That's not true', or 'I'm actually a generous person'.

"What we all tend to complain about most in other people are those things we don't like about ourselves."

William Wharton

(If it's a friend or close family member, you can always return to the topic later – when you are not so indignant – and have an honest conversation about it. Ask what's behind the criticism: 'Are you angry about someone or something else?'.)

What about unexpected criticism – how do I stop myself bursting into tears?

In most situations where you are criticised, you will have been (at least half) expecting it. This is because you will already know that your boss/colleague tends to criticise your work or that your friend/partner is invariably critical about you. If you create something and show it to someone else then you can expect to receive criticism because you are inviting it.

Confident people actually invite criticism. High-achieving students at school and university are often dismissive of praise and want to know exactly how they can improve their work.

Similarly, if you are in a relationship that is going through a difficult patch you may want to have a serious and frank discussion about what you can do to improve it. This takes courage, but many relationships founder because people **assume** that the other person knows what annoys them.

Most disagreements arise from unspoken assumptions. Sometimes the other person is not sufficiently assertive to articulate their criticism – you may need to help them out: 'I know I have been out a lot recently. Is it annoying you?' Even if you haven't hit on the right thing, it will open up a discussion and give them a chance to say what they think.

Once you have learned how to react to criticism – and had plenty of practice – you will be able to respond to unexpected criticism in exactly the same way as when you are prepared for it.

Meanwhile, here are a few responses that you can use for those times when you are totally unprepared for that hurtful comment.

1. When someone makes a comment about your appearance:

   'You've had your hair cut', just say, 'Right', and change the subject. Do not say, 'Yes, do you like it?'.

   Or, 'Don't you think that's a bit young for you?' Just say, '**No**', and change the subject (your tone of voice will make the difference between an aggressive no and an assertive no). You can even assertively say, 'Yes', with a smile, if you agree with them.

   Or, 'Don't you think that's a bit too short/makes you look fat/a low neckline?' etc. Say firmly, but kindly, 'No, I don't'. Do not get drawn into an argument: repeat the phrase if necessary. (Again, 'Yes' is fine – as long as you are not apologetic about it and don't add an anxious explanation.)

2. If someone makes a derogatory comment about some work that you have done, e.g. decorating:

   'You seem to have missed a bit here', or 'Oops, what went wrong there?'. Either ignore their comment as though you haven't heard, or tell them how you feel:

   'That's not like you to make such an unkind remark.' (You could add, 'Aren't you feeling well?' but I think we may be bordering on sarcasm here.) You can use this for offensive comments on your appearance too. Don't fall into the trap of self-deprecation.

3. If someone criticises your behaviour:

   Try humour in the form of exaggerated self-deprecation; this works especially well with moaning children:

   'You're so mean not letting me have … ' or 'Why can't I have … ?' Just say, 'Because I'm such a dreadful/horrible/mean parent', and laugh.

   I once heard a teacher criticise another for not having detailed lesson plans (which he wanted to borrow). When asked why she didn't have any, her laughing reply was:

'Because I'm such an appalling teacher.' Of course the other person then protested and tried to backtrack.

HOWEVER: it may be difficult for you to always respond assertively when someone catches you unawares. Don't feel too bad if you burst into tears or get angry – you're only human, and it's a natural reaction to be defensive. This is particularly true if you are already tired, depressed or not feeling well.

Even when you have been assertive in your response, you may still feel upset afterwards. Telling a close friend about it may help, but don't let yourself continue to brood about it. Know that you have done your best, and move on.

What about the bully?

Once you have mastered the assertiveness techniques in this book, you are not likely to be bullied. The bully has a sixth sense for your areas of vulnerability and uses this to boost their own sense of self-esteem. Being assertive doesn't mean that people will stop being mean to you or stop making cruel remarks, but it means that you will be able to deal with them and not let them reduce you to a quivering wreck or a state of abject fury.

Never try to pacify the bully or get round them by being nice to them – they will know they have power over you. If they are strangers, ignore them (but in a confident way – not with your head down, avoiding eye contact).

- Use humour. Laughing at their comments (and getting other people to join in if possible) is the most assertive response. It won't endear you to the bully but you're not trying to get them to like you.

- Use the trick of *negative assertion* – agree with them: 'Yes, I have', or 'I'll bear that in mind' (don't repeat the taunt).

- If you are being bullied at work, find your company's bullying policy and follow the procedures. You have the right to do this.

- If you are being bullied by family or friends, choose a time and ask them to listen to you for ten minutes. Explain what you have to say calmly, honestly and without exaggeration. Begin with 'I've been feeling ... I'd like you to ... '.

- For your own mental health you may want to decide what your 'or else' is going to be if they don't stop. You don't have to tell them this, but it is useful to have already decided what steps you are going to take if the bullying doesn't stop.

Giving constructive criticism

When we ask our students to rank how difficult they find different aspects of assertiveness, giving and receiving criticism are always listed as the hardest. Most people think that receiving criticism is more difficult than giving it, but when questioned more closely this usually turns out to mean that they simply avoid criticising others. In other words, it is so difficult for an unassertive person to criticise, they just keep quiet and don't mention things that irritate or upset them.

Remember: you have the right to ask someone to change their behaviour if it hurts, annoys or offends you.

Think about recent occasions when you have had a grievance or problem with someone. What did you do about it?

Aggressive response: You got angry and confronted them with a torrent of abuse.

Indirect aggressive response: You made snide/sarcastic/mean remarks about the person behind their back.

Passive response: You avoided dealing with them directly but found yourself moaning to other people about the situation.

Assertive response: You expressed your feelings about the behaviour.

It sounds simple, but your inability to criticise someone else in an assertive, non-aggressive way can be understood now you have examined your own reaction to any hint of criticism. We do not want to 'nag' or criticise because we are afraid of the other person's reaction.

So what's the consequence of saying nothing?

Not mentioning things, or not standing up for yourself, in order to keep the peace, will not make your feelings go away. In fact, burying negative feelings allows the resentment to fester and grow.

The longer you ignore seemingly trivial hurts and upsets the more they tend to build up and then boil over with rage or bitterness. Trying to put a brave face on it, by pushing your feelings to one side and continuing to be pleasant, is a recipe for tension, stress and consequent health problems.

Let's imagine your partner says: 'You're not much of a cook, are you?'. You are hurt because you've been working late, bought a ready meal, prepared and served it out without any help. You don't say anything.

At the weekend you are out together and he meets some friends but fails to introduce you or include you in the conversation. You don't say anything.

You remind him about some trivial household task (like putting the rubbish out) but he forgets and goes out. You have to do it in your nightclothes. You don't say anything.

You're supposed to be saving but he buys a boxed set of DVDs and suddenly you explode with anger. He is confused: 'What's the matter with you? They didn't cost that much.'

If you recognise this tendency to let little things pass but find yourself feeling resentful each time, have a go at being more assertively outspoken in future.

Aim for consistency in your reaction towards others

Harbouring resentment will undermine both personal and work relationships. Some people find it easy to criticise friends and family but allow their work colleagues to get away with poor behaviour or disrespectful comments (and for others the reverse is true).

> "Harbouring resentment will undermine both personal and work relationships."

Why do you find it easier to criticise in some situations than others? If it is just that you know you can say what you want to your parent/partner/child – whereas someone at work might be offended – then you might need to examine the reason for this. Not caring what you say to someone – because they are family and can't do anything about it – makes you a bit of a bully. Conversely, not saying what you want to because you are afraid that your criticism may cause upset or make people dislike you is a bit cowardly.

If you believe that you have the right to request a change in someone's offensive behaviour, then you have that right both at home and outside the home. The techniques for giving criticism are the same – whomever it is that you are saying it to. Don't let fear stop you doing or saying what you know is right.

Help other people to be assertive so that you have a win–win situation

Giving constructive criticism shows that you value the other person and your relationship with them. Direct, open and specific feedback to others about their behaviour can be helpful and lead to a better working or loving relationship. Of course, the other person may not be assertive and may react badly to criticism. This doesn't mean that you should shy away from what you want to say – just that you have to think carefully about what you do want to say and how you are going to say it.

- Before criticising someone, check your motivation. It is fine just to complain about something (for example the food in a restaurant), but if you have a specific change in mind make sure that you are flexible and allow the other person some respect. Your intention is to get them to change their behaviour – not to humiliate them.

- Choose the time and the place; although it is best to say something immediately, it may not be appropriate – particularly if there are other people around. Most people would be defensive if they thought other people could hear. (This is one of the reasons why some children continue to behave badly in class after they have been told off.)

- Don't let things build up, thinking that things will change without you having to say anything – they rarely do, they just get worse. When you can feel someone's behaviour beginning to annoy you it is best to tackle it as soon as possible. Your responsibility to the other person is to prevent your own resentment towards them from building up. This means that you have respect for their rights, as the consequence of ignoring their behaviour will just be detrimental to you both.

- If even after your best efforts to spell out your grievance nothing has changed, you may need to review the situation. Is it something they can change or is it their personality? Some people react badly to criticism and may need more help to know what to do.

Six steps for giving criticism

1. Try to say some good points alongside the criticism

This is a particularly effective method with people who don't take criticism well. 'I appreciate the way that you have been prepared to work late but ... '.

(You can use the PNP sandwich: saying something positive, then negative, then positive. Be careful though; if you use this formula too rigidly and too often people may recognise what you are doing and wait resignedly for the 'but'.)

2. **Criticise the behaviour – not the person**

Remember what you have learned about receiving criticism: that it is not acceptable to label the person: 'You're mean' or 'You're a selfish person.'

So, instead of saying, 'You're totally unreliable', try saying, 'You've been late twice this week'.

3. **Express your feelings about their behaviour**

Instead of saying, 'You don't seem to care about anyone's feelings', say, 'I was upset when you spoke to me in that way in front of everyone.'

Only say this if you can trust the person and want to improve your relationship with them.

4. **Shut up and listen to them**

Again, remember what it felt like to be on the receiving end of criticism: you wanted to explain and justify your behaviour. There is a tendency when giving criticism to feel self-righteous and to go on and on long after you have made your point.

Given the chance, the other person may give you some information that you didn't know and that changes your view. Check this by repeating what they say: 'Have I got this right? You're saying that … '.

5. **Ask for a specific change of behaviour and seek their agreement**

If you just moan or you are too vague in your criticism the other person might not understand how exactly you want them to change. If they accept what you are saying (which is far more likely if your tone is not aggressive), then ask for their suggestions for improvement.

Instead of saying, 'You never help around the house', be specific: 'You haven't cooked a meal once this week. Which days would you be able to make the meal next week?'.

6. **Talk about the consequences**

If the person is reacting badly to your criticism and completely ignores what you have to say, you need to decide what will happen if nothing changes. (This is like the 'or else' that was mentioned as a useful strategy when dealing with bullies.) You are not threatening – just taking control of the situation. You can decide what you will do without actually stating the negative consequences:

'If you continue to be late I will be left with no option but to take this matter further.'

Or if it is a friend who always turns up late to see you:

'I'm so fed up with you being late (I think in future I'll wait until you ring me before I set off).'

If the person listens to what you have to say, and accepts your point, state the positive consequences and end on an optimistic note:

'If you cook, it will mean you can choose what we have to eat. I'm really happy that we've been able to sort this out.'

Top tips

- If you have spent most of your life being unable to give and receive criticism, you are not going to be able to do it overnight. It takes practice.
- Don't try to do everything all at once.
- Learn to accept less than perfection.
- Don't beat yourself up if you get it wrong.
- One difference between aggression and assertion is respect for the other person.
- Say everything as briefly as possible.
- If the other person argues, just repeat what you have said.
- If you are nervous about a possible confrontation, get someone to role-play it with you.

- Be honest.
- Don't store up resentment – tell them now.
- It's much more difficult to be assertive if you are tired, depressed or unwell.
- If you can't think of the right reply at the time, you can always say something later – if it's still bothering you.
- You may feel upset after giving criticism that is badly received; it doesn't mean you were wrong to say it.

Part

2

'Courage is the first of human virtues because it
makes all other virtues possible.'

Aristotle

Putting it into practice

Having studied the various aspects of assertive behaviour, we will now look at how these can be put into practice. If you examine the answers that you gave to the questions in the quiz in Chapter 1, you will have realised in which areas you are least, and most, assertive. We look at these areas in different chapters in Part 2. The case studies cover all aspects of assertiveness, from saying 'no' to receiving criticism. You will also see from the case studies some suggestions about how the situations in the quiz could be handled in an assertive way.

When you have understood and learned the ways to change your behaviour and become more assertive, you will be ready for the final stage of your journey – decision making. Being able to make good decisions – decisions that you have thought about carefully and know that you will not regret – is all part of becoming assertive. Just as there are clear and simple steps that you can make to help yourself become more assertive in your dealings with other people, there are also logical steps that can be learned to help you make effective decisions. In Chapter 13 we look closely at these steps and see them in practice by referring to the case studies in previous chapters.

Chapter

5

'All happy families resemble one another, each unhappy family is unhappy in its own way.'

Anna Karenina, Leo Tolstoy

How to be assertive with your family

Look back now to the quiz in Chapter 1: how assertive are you with your family? How did this compare to your score with friends or at work? Some people find that being assertive with their family is easy but might find it difficult to complain about poor service. You may realise that it is easy for you to be assertive with some members of your family (for example, your children or sister), but others are able to reduce you to rage or a feeling of helplessness.

In this chapter we examine some of the situations described in the quiz and look at how they could be handled in an assertive way.

Asking for what you want

Moira works as a sales rep for a local pharmaceutical company. She has three sons (aged 10, 13 and 15) and a new partner, Rob – who often gets home late. She feels that she takes on the burden of most of the housework because she gets home first (and because she always did it before Rob came on the scene).

Moira is becoming increasingly aware, and resentful, of the way her partner fails to help. She complains about her lot to others, but tends to make sarcastic hints or to be withdrawn at home – as it is easier than getting into a confrontation. Rob is usually tired when he gets home. He feels that he does his bit by taking out the rubbish, washing the car and occasionally mowing the lawn. He prefers to relax on a weekend, and usually goes to see his local team play football on a Saturday afternoon and often goes out drinking with his friends.

Can you identify Moira's behaviour from the definitions in Chapter 1? It is passive–aggressive behaviour: she avoids conflict by doing everything herself but reveals her anger in her moods and sarcasm – instead of tackling the problem and dealing honestly with the things that are annoying her.

Moira has tried in the past to get Rob and her sons to help more in the house but has found it only lasts for a while and then they sink back into their old ways. She has fallen into the trap that many parents fall into: continuing to play the role of the mother of small children long after that role is needed. It has become a habit for her to do everything, and it suits the rest of the family.

Moira may also feel guilty; she has separated from the children's father and introduced a new man into the household. She is trying her best to keep the peace by not asking anything of anyone. She may be grateful to Rob for accepting her ready-made family and this makes her reluctant to ask more of him.

Everyone has a right to be happy

Often we feel unable to ask for help because, deep down, we feel we don't deserve it. If we accept that this is our lot in life and just strive to keep everyone else around us happy, we build up resentment that inevitably erupts.

The assertive thing to do would be to acknowledge that these anxieties exist *and* realise that we have the right to ask for what we want and the right to be happy too. We would express our needs and ensure that they are met without being afraid of the consequences.

Assertive *ACTION*

The first step to asserting your needs is to take some time to **decide what it is you actually want**. This is harder than it seems, which is why we often fall into passive–aggressive traps. Make sure that you think carefully about what you want as the final outcome. It's no good asking your partner to take over the cooking at the weekends if this is what you most enjoy doing, or if you wouldn't be able to relax if someone else is doing it. To help clarify your needs, try writing a list of all the things you would like help with and then decide which of these things you could imagine relinquishing to someone else.

"To help clarify your needs, try writing a list of all the things you would like help with."

When you are ready to voice your feelings and your needs, **take absolute ownership of this in the language you use.** Rather than 'You make me feel', say 'I feel'. Moira might say, 'I feel upset that I do most of the housework', for example. And when you say what you want, say exactly what you want – name it precisely. Moira could say: 'I would like you to cook a meal every Thursday night.'

If you really don't know the details of the help you want, you could **invite ideas**: 'I'm exhausted at the weekend having to do all the cooking and cleaning, have you got any ideas about how you could help?' And be sure to only ask for one thing at a time – your message can become cluttered if you ask for too much at once, and change is always more palatable in small doses.

Timing and body language are also key. Consider when would be the best time, the most constructive time, to engage your audience. After a stressful day at work or late at night are not good times for most people. Perhaps you could first find out when would be a good time to talk – it's important you set the conversation up as a positive discussion, not a negative complaint.

Be sure that your body language is in keeping with a positive, solution-focused outlook – no folded arms or wringing hands! **Try to have an open gesture that invites discussion** rather than a hands-on-hips stance that suggests that you are expecting opposition and are prepared for a fight. Make sure that you smile and don't look too serious. Your aim is to sort out something that has been bothering you, not to get into another argument. Your tone of voice is all-important: it needs to be quietly self-assured, not a whine, a meek whisper or loud and aggressive.

Finally, **avoid giving up too easily**. You have made your request and it has been heard, but it doesn't mean that change will happen, or continue to happen. You may have to battle habits of a lifetime and you will have to decide what you are going to say and do if there is no cooperation – 'I feel let down after what we discussed last week' or 'I've noticed that you have not been … as you agreed, so I've decided to … ', for example. In this last example, you don't have to say what you have decided to do as a next step; it is not a threat but a promise to yourself (but make sure that what you have decided isn't detrimental to you).

Remember

Don't forget to thank and praise when you have achieved what you want – *everyone* appreciates a 'thank you' and praise.

Saying 'no'

David's mother, Gloria, has been a widow for two years after being happily married for over 40 years. She has a daughter who lives abroad and another son who has a young family. David lives nearby and Gloria telephones him most days, usually with some pretext for him to call round and see her.

David knows that his mother is lonely but he has recently started a new relationship. He finds himself getting increasingly irritated by his mother's dependence on him but doesn't want to hurt her feelings.

David feels sorry for his mother and is trying to help her by doing the jobs that his father would have done at home. At first he was happy to do this as he too missed his father and enjoyed sharing the memories that they both had of him. However, what began as a pleasure has now become a routine that he is finding difficult to change. He would like to spend more time on his new relationship, but his mother expects him to call round when she asks. He is passively doing what his mother wants and it is making his new relationship difficult.

In a predicament like this you have two choices: you can decide that you would rather continue in the way that you have been, or that you are going to do something about it. Whatever you decide, there will be consequences, but it is better to make a decision than just to let things slide and take your frustration out on other people.

David realised that he would be annoyed with his mother if his new relationship was affected by her reliance on him. He also knew that he didn't want to upset his mother. He wanted to tell his mother that he wouldn't be able to see her so often.

Assertive *ACTION*

If you feel anxious, nervous or guilty about saying 'no' to a close family member then begin by saying so: '**I feel anxious** about saying this to you because I don't want to upset you … ' or 'I've been plucking up the courage to say this but I really don't want to … ' or 'I feel guilty saying this but I'm not going to … '.

If the person objects then say very simply: '**Sorry, no, I can't …**'. You don't have to give an explanation. If the person tries to persuade you, just repeat the same words. Sometimes you may have to repeat yourself five or six times before they get the message. Once they have accepted that you are not going to be persuaded, then you can offer a compromise that suits you both well: 'But I could come round on Saturday.'

Of course, the other person is likely to be resentful that you have not acquiesced to their demands in your usual way. They may get angry or fall out with you. **You are not responsible for their behaviour** and you can see that it is manipulative to behave in this way. If you give in and do what they want, then you have to accept the consequences. David realised that as long as his mother continued to dominate his life, his new relationship would not stand a chance.

Remember

Be aware of your body language and tone of voice. Just because you are saying 'no' does not mean that you have to be aggressive or loud. Be kind: this is a member of your family and you want to maintain a good relationship.

Receiving criticism

Tiffany and Paul have recently bought a new flat, which they are decorating and furnishing on a limited budget. Paul's older sister, Pam, often comes to visit them with her two children. Her husband, Jack, a property developer, visits less frequently but when he does he tends to criticise their efforts. He makes 'jokes' about their decorating and says things like, 'Those shelves won't stay up long'.

Tiffany resents Jack's comments and dreads his visits. She doesn't want to say anything in case she upsets Paul's sister and so she behaves in a passive manner. Paul is also annoyed by Jack's behaviour but he is more aggressive and has had rows with Jack in the past. Now Paul reacts by shutting himself in the study whenever his brother-in-law turns up – which simply leaves Tiffany to deal with the situation on her own.

This kind of criticism serves no purpose other than to put the other person down – or to make the critic feel good. Sometimes people do genuinely think that they are being funny and are dismayed when it is pointed out to them how hurtful their comments are. Jack, however, is a bully and seems to enjoy the fact that he can so easily upset his brother-in-law.

Assertive *ACTION*

The best way of dealing with someone like Jack is with humour. This is difficult when you are feeling angry, but Tiffany and Paul could actually prepare for his visit and plan what they are going to say to his inevitable criticism. They could **agree a strategy and role-play the situation**. This may seem strange if you have never done it before, but actually trying out some funny comments, practising the way you are going to stand and even the expression on your face, can be a useful way of dealing with a situation that is becoming intolerable.

"The best way of dealing with someone like Jack is with humour."

One way of doing this is to **invite criticism**. So, after decorating, the couple might open the door to Jack and with a laugh say: 'OK. Let's get it over with: tell us what we've done wrong.' You have to be careful not to be sarcastic; sarcasm is always aggressive and is a tactic of the bully. Your tone of voice and stance may betray how you are really feeling. To stand up to a bully like Jack you need to be able to look at him, relax your shoulders and speak with confidence.

You could try **negative assertion** – where you agree with the criticism in a strong, jovial manner. 'Yes, we're just beginners. I expect we'll be moving house by the time we get the hang of it.' But make sure that you do say this in a robust way – if you say it in a hesitant, self-deprecating manner then the bully will have won and will continue to bait you at every visit.

The intention of a bully is to hurt and to humiliate, but if the comments aren't having the desired effect they will, eventually, give up. **Try laughing** at such critical comments and say pleasantly: 'If you can't say anything nice – don't say anything.' It is easier to laugh and to make fun of the bully if you have someone with you. If you do have a difficult relative then try to persuade a friend to be with you for the visit, and brief them on your plan of action.

Don't try to pacify or to argue with a bully. As soon as you react in a defensive or aggressive way they will immediately realise that they have won. They will continue to use sarcasm and cruel comments because they are having the desired effect – your discomfort. Avoiding the bully by retreating to another room also shows someone like Jack that they have the power. Paul's behaviour is just cowardly and won't solve anything.

Remember

Family members aren't going to go away. Either you have to develop a thick skin and not let their comments get to you or you must decide to say something. It is much better to deal with the situation rather than spending your life trying to appease someone or avoiding a confrontation.

"It is much better to deal with the situation rather than spending your life trying to appease someone."

Receiving a compliment

Donna is a single mother with one child. She works full time as a midwife, is a school governor and an active member of a political party. On a recent visit to her parents, her father told her that they were very proud of her: they admired the way that she puts so much energy into improving the lives of others as well as being a loving and attentive mother.

Because Donna was unaccustomed to receiving praise from her father she was immediately dismissive. She laughed and told him not to be so silly – she was no different to anyone else. Making a flippant remark when someone has complimented you is often a defence reaction to cover up your embarrassment. Rejecting a compliment can be hurtful to the other person and probably means that they won't try it again.

Assertive *ACTION*

The ideal response to this kind of thoughtful compliment would be: 'I appreciate you telling me this. You've made me feel good about myself.'

Remember

Accept compliments with a smile, not a frown. Don't deny them, however embarrassed you feel – just say 'thank you'.

Giving a compliment

Natalie has a 12-year-old daughter, Rosie. Natalie was bullied as a child and still suffers from low self-esteem. She is anxious that Rosie doesn't suffer in the same way and constantly praises her. Recently she has noticed that this seems to irritate Rosie and that although Rosie is quick to detect any hint of criticism, she seems to disregard Natalie's compliments and admiring comments.

Most parents want their children to feel good about themselves and they know that praising them is more likely to encourage them to work harder or to practise more often. However, indiscriminate compliments and praise can have unfortunate consequences. Sometimes parents praise their child because they want them to do well in an area in which they themselves wanted to achieve. This can result in the child thinking that they have a talent in an area in which, in fact, they have little aptitude.

The reason why Rosie takes notice of the criticism and disregards the compliments is because the criticism she receives is usually more specific – 'You're not holding your violin correctly' or 'Your handwriting is very untidy' – whereas the compliments she receives are constant and vague.

Assertive *ACTION*

The effect of general compliments is that they become meaningless. It's OK to tell someone that their work is good or that they look very nice but it is better if you **pick out something specific that you genuinely admire**. 'I like the way you managed to make the poem rhyme without making it obvious' is better than 'That's a good poem'.

With adults the same thing applies. In the previous example, Donna's father's compliment was thoughtful and honest. This is the kind of compliment that is worth giving and that is treasured and remembered.

Remember

People often forget to give compliments to family members, as though being related makes gratitude and praise irrelevant. Giving sincere and specific compliments is a good way to promote family harmony and to encourage self-esteem.

Top tips

- Every time you disregard your feelings you are, in fact, simply storing them up for a later date.
- Most family members will be a part of your life for a long time so it is usually better to be assertive rather than spending your life avoiding confrontations.
- There is, of course, no guarantee of success – you can't change the behaviour of other people but you can change yourself.
- You will, however, find that by changing your behaviour, other people in the family will react differently towards you: if you start standing up for yourself people will stop taking you for granted.

Chapter

'No person is your friend who demands your silence,
or denies your right to grow.'

Alice Walker

How to be assertive with your friends

How did you score in the friends section of the quiz? It may be that you have happy, supportive and equal friendships that never cause you a problem. But, often, being assertive with friends can be just as difficult and complex as dealing with different members of your family.

We assume that we can 'be ourselves' with our friends, but sometimes with friends we can find ourselves cast in a role that we no longer enjoy. Often this just means that we have settled into a pattern of behaviour that needs to be broken.

In this chapter we will look at various situations that may occur with friends and suggest some assertive ways of dealing with them.

Saying 'no'

Deborah has lived next door to Sharazard for many years. Deborah's children are away at university but Sharazard has a young son, who has special needs. One Saturday morning Sharazard knocks at Deborah's door and asks her if she would be able to babysit the following Saturday because her husband has arranged for them to go out for their 20th wedding anniversary.

Deborah has been looking forward to her school reunion, which is on the same night. She tries to say no but Sharazard bursts into tears and says her babysitter is ill and she has found it difficult to get anyone else because of her son's special needs. She reminds Deborah of how long they have known each other and says that her son has always liked Deborah. In the end Deborah agrees to babysit.

How do you imagine that you would have reacted? This is a typical role-play exercise that we use with assertiveness classes. Most people in the class say that they would give in and do the babysitting. Even when they are asked to say 'no' in a role-play, some people are still worn down by a persuasive partner and end up saying 'yes'. We are used to putting our own wishes second and we so want to be useful and liked.

The trouble is that it is often easier to acquiesce than to be assertive. Saying 'yes' becomes a habit. People expect it from you. When you try to say 'no' they are cross and try every technique in their power to persuade you to change your mind. This can range from anger to withdrawal, tears and reminders of your debt to them.

"Saying 'yes' becomes a habit. People expect it from you."

You have rights too

The person making the request feels they have the right to ask you because you are a friend – which is true – but you also have the right to say 'no'. Of course you are entitled to respond in whatever way you want when someone asks you for a favour. There are many times in life when we do things we don't want to do in order to be kind; assertive people are just as kind as anyone else. However, if you find yourself *always* saying 'yes' when you'd rather say 'no', and you feel that people take advantage of you, then it may be time to take stock and to learn how to say 'no'.

Assertive *ACTION*

When a friend asks for a favour and there is no reason not to help, then, of course, there is no problem. It feels good to do things for other people, and in the best friendships this is reciprocated. Conversely, if the first thought that crosses your mind is, 'No, I really don't want to do that', and there is no doubt in your mind, then you just say, 'Sorry, no, I can't.' **You don't have to give an explanation.**

But usually it's not a clear-cut decision. Deborah could do the babysitting – she just preferred to do something else. If people are used to you being a pushover, they are not going to give up without a fight. They might ask you what it is that you are doing that is so important. Don't, at this stage, tell them. Whatever you say they will come up with alternatives for you and you will simply get into a different argument.

So when someone tries to persuade you, **just repeat the phrase that you first used**: 'Sorry, no, I can't', or, 'Sorry, I'm not going to be able to do it this time.' Sometimes you need to repeat this four or five times before they get the message and give up.

Whenever you are asked to do something and your first thought is, 'No, I could do it but I'd rather ... ', **ask for time to think about it**. Sometimes this only means a few minutes – even when you are on the telephone you can ring them back a few minutes later. So Deborah could have said: 'Can you give me some time to think about it? I'll let you know by this afternoon'.

If you find yourself slipping into your old habits and saying 'yes' and then later kicking yourself and wishing that you had said 'no', then say that you have changed your mind. Simply say, 'I'm sorry, I've changed my mind and I'm not going to be able to ... '. It is harder once you have said 'yes', but as an assertive person you know that **changing your mind is OK** – it doesn't make you a bad person.

Don't forget to **check your body language**; don't look down or shift your feet and hands about uncomfortably. Say it clearly and pleasantly. There may be tears, but you can comfort them without letting yourself be manipulated. It sometimes helps if you say: 'I've given this some thought but ...' as then they know they are not likely to persuade you to change your mind. When they have accepted that you are not going to give in, *then* you can suggest a compromise: 'I could babysit for you on the Friday night if you were able to change the booking.' People are always resistant to a new idea and they may be angry that you haven't agreed. Just say: 'Anyway, think about it. The offer's there.'

Make a decision that, for the next few weeks, whenever you feel yourself about to say 'yes' to something you have doubts about, pause, examine your motives and decide if you are just doing it because you are afraid of not being liked. If so, be brave and either say 'no' or that you'd like some time to think about it. Notice the ways that are used to try to persuade you. It will take some practice before you get used to it, but in the end you will find that you are treated less like a doormat and more like a valued friend.

Role-play

With all difficult situations (ones that may have been troubling you for some time), the best thing you can do is to get someone to role-play the situation with you. So if a friend is always asking you for favours and you want to say 'no' but find yourself saying 'yes', get someone to role-play the part of the friend and practise saying: 'No, sorry, I can't.' Role-play is a useful technique for most of the situations we have described in this book. If you can't get anyone to play, then practise yourself in front of a mirror.

Some people find it easier to say 'no' on the telephone. Try practising with cold callers: just say pleasantly, 'No, thanks, I'm not interested', and put the phone down – before they begin their spiel.

Remember

The net effect of doing something that you don't want to do may be that you please one person but build up resentment, which inevitably will have a negative effect on your friendship.

Giving criticism

Danny and Tom have been friends since university. They are now in their thirties and continue to meet occasionally to play snooker and to go to the gym. Although they both have similarly well-paid jobs, Tom is becoming aware of how often he ends up paying for things for both of them. Recently Danny has also started borrowing money, but Tom is reluctant to mention it to him as he doesn't want to spoil their friendship.

Tom knows that Danny has always been careful with his money, but Tom has recently started saving for a deposit for a flat and it annoys him that Danny suggests that they meet but then never seems to have any money. So far he has borrowed only small amounts, and Tom keeps telling himself that it is not worth losing his friendship over a tenner. He's tried making a joke of it when it is Danny's turn to buy a round, but Danny seems oblivious to his hints.

The subject of money can often cause difficulties in families and with friends. It is a touchy subject that people don't like to talk about because they don't want to appear mean. However, Tom now notices Danny's behaviour every time they are together and it is affecting his attitude towards his friend. Instead of tackling the problem, he is beginning to find excuses to avoid meeting Danny.

Tom is being passive and risks losing a friend because he doesn't know how best to say what he is thinking. Giving criticism can show that you value the friendship – but you have to make sure that it is constructive and not just an insult designed to make you feel better.

"Giving criticism can show that you value the friendship."

Assertive *ACTION*

First of all you have to **decide what exactly you are criticising** and then how you are going to say it. It needs careful thought as there may be a lot at stake (a long-term friendship in this case), not least someone's self-esteem. It is usually a good idea to disclose how nervous or anxious you are feeling about the conversation. If you find it difficult to express your feelings, it might be best to start off with some kind of warning about what you are going to say: 'I've been worried about saying this to you', or 'I don't want this to affect our friendship but … '.

Say something positive like, 'We've been friends for a long time … ' or, 'I always enjoy … ', then say what it is that is annoying you. Remember not to generalise – **it is the behaviour you are criticising – not the person**. So instead of saying, 'You're very mean with your money', Tom could say, 'I seem to end up paying for more than my share these days'.

Then **give the other person a chance to reply**. Don't be surprised if they are defensive and deny it. Most people find it difficult to accept criticism and it would be unusual and surprising if they replied, 'You're right – I'll change my behaviour in future'. It's more likely that they will say, 'That's not true. Last week I bought you … '. Try not to get into an argument at this point. You've said what you wanted to say and they've heard it. Don't go on about it – just listen to what they say.

If you tend to be aggressive, try sitting down before delivering your criticism and make sure that your tone of voice stays quiet and reasonable. If you tend to be passive, then stay standing, keep your head up, make eye contact and speak clearly and confidently. They may be angry, upset or resentful, but this does not mean you were wrong to speak out. **You can't help how the other person reacts** but you can make sure that you don't become defensive or aggressive in response. It can be quite exhausting if you aren't used to being assertive, but it becomes easier with practice.

Finally, try to **end on a lighter, more positive note**: 'I'm glad I've been able to talk to you about this', or, 'Now, how about buying me that drink? You still owe me a tenner.' If you have been thinking about this encounter for some time it may have been difficult but, whatever the outcome, you will feel relieved and probably elated that you have spoken out.

Remember

Just because you have spoken your mind doesn't guarantee success. Expressing yourself assertively doesn't mean that the other person will change – it simply means that you are no longer afraid.

Receiving criticism

Let's look at the case study from Danny's point of view. As far as he's concerned, he's just gone for a game of snooker with an old friend and suddenly he's been accused of being mean. He may be aware of this – people who are 'careful with money' often see other, more generous people as extravagant or even show-offs. Because Tom is always first at the bar he just accepts it. Tom's generosity suits him and there has been no reason to change since Tom has never mentioned it, apart from a few vague jokes.

Assertive *ACTION*

When you receive criticism from a friend, take a deep breath and **listen carefully** to what they are saying – it takes courage for someone to tell you what has been on their mind. This is a friend, so you have to trust that their comments are for your benefit or to improve the friendship. Recognise that your initial reaction will be to be defensive and try to keep an open mind. Think whether someone has ever said this to you before.

Paraphrase the criticism so that you are sure that you understand exactly what they mean. So in this case Danny might say, 'Are you saying that you always pay for me?', to which Tom might reply, 'No, I'm just saying that I seem to end up paying for more than my fair share.' Once you realise exactly what they mean then you have to seriously consider whether or not the criticism is valid.

Resist the temptation to be indignant and to justify your behaviour – that can come later. For the moment you just have to either accept or reject the criticism. If you can see that it is true then say so: 'Yes, you do tend to pay more often than I do.' Once you have admitted it you can justify yourself if you want: 'I didn't realise it was a problem. You always seemed to enjoy paying.' Or perhaps: 'I'm sorry. I've got money problems at the moment but I didn't want to tell you.'

Say what you intend to do about it: 'I promise I'll pay for my share in future', or ask for help: 'It's become a habit for me – can you just remind me in future?' If you don't think you'll be able to change (or you are not prepared to) then say so: 'I know I've always been careful with my money and I don't think I'm prepared to change.' It is then the other person's decision to choose what to do about it.

If you don't accept the criticism as valid then say so – in a non-aggressive way: 'That's not true. I don't ... '. If you're not sure, ask them to repeat it: 'Can you just say that again?' (This quite often results in a toned-down version of what they said before.) If it's partly true then agree but qualify it: 'It's true I'm not always first at the bar but I usually pay my way.' Be careful that your indignation does not make you aggressive – keep your voice down and a pleasant expression on your face (but probably not a smile).

Remember

If you are genuinely mystified by the criticism, try applying similar words to your critic. It's strange, but quite often people accuse others of their own faults.

Giving and receiving compliments

“An acquaintance that begins with a compliment is sure to develop into a real friendship.”

Oscar Wilde

Deborah goes to her school reunion and meets a couple of her old friends. They make a fuss of her and say that she has lost weight since they last saw her. One friend admires the dress that she is wearing and says that the colour really suits her. Deborah immediately says that they all look good, that the dress was only cheap and that she's got loads more weight to lose.

Have you ever reacted like this when a friend gives you a compliment? However you feel about yourself, do you have a tendency to be self-deprecating and to deflect any compliments or praise?

"Do you have a tendency to be self-deprecating and to deflect any compliments or praise?"

'This old thing'

Whenever someone gives you a compliment and you try to avert it by saying something critical about yourself you are actually showing them a lack of respect. Giving a compliment can be quite an effort for some people and it is certainly a sign of generosity. By contradicting them you are throwing their kindness back at them.

By saying, 'Do you think so?' or 'It's just something I threw on' (when actually you have spent ages getting ready), you are being dishonest and implying that your friend can't have much taste if she likes it. Quite often compliments are just used as an ice-breaker when friends first meet, which is fine, but the compliment Deborah received was specific – they had noticed her new dress.

Assertive *ACTION*

The best response to a compliment is to **look pleased and simply thank the person**. Deborah could have said: 'Thanks very much. It's the first time I've worn it so I'm glad you like it too.'

If you genuinely want to give a compliment to a friend (rather than just use it as a pleasantry when first meeting), then it's better not to return a compliment as soon as you receive one. Deborah said, 'You all look good too', almost as an involuntary response to being told that she looked good. This is the accepted response – and it is almost impolite not to react like this – but in terms of giving a compliment it is pretty meaningless. It's best to **wait for an opportunity later** and then also to give a specific compliment that you genuinely mean – otherwise it just seems as if you are saying it automatically because you were given one.

When responding to a compliment you could say something like, 'Thank you very much. You've made my day', or 'Thanks for telling me that. You've made me feel good about myself'. This makes the other person feel pleased too and there will be a generally positive atmosphere that can set you up for the rest of the day.

Start right now noticing your initial response when someone compliments you. Make sure that you smile and look pleased to receive the compliment. Also start noticing other people's reactions to praise and compliments. You will be amazed by how often people are unable to accept what is being said to them and will immediately begin to deny it or be self-deprecating. If the person you are complimenting isn't assertive and says, 'Oh no, it was nothing', that's fine. You can't make other people respond to you the way you'd like them to – **you can only change your own behaviour.**

Remember

Give compliments to your friends about the things that they do and say – not just about their appearance. Think about what you like about them – and tell them.

Top tips

- Assertive friends can speak their minds without being afraid that they will fall out with each other.

- They can have healthy disagreements and are able to negotiate and compromise.

- They do things for each other because they want to – not because they want to be liked.

- They know that if their request is turned down it doesn't mean that their friend doesn't like them any more.

- Good friendships are equal friendships, and only equals can both give and accept each other's criticism.

- When you are assertive you are able to tell your friends what you like and admire about them and to accept the same from them.

- Being assertive with friends may be difficult because you (and they) have got used to the role that you play in the friendship.

Chapter 7

'My grandfather once told me that there were two kinds of people: those who do the work and those who take the credit. He told me to try to be in the first group; there was much less competition.'

Indira Gandhi

How to be assertive at work

Many people find being assertive at work more difficult than being assertive with friends or family members. You will have known most members of your family all your life and you have chosen your friends because you like them and they like you. The people you work with, however, are just individuals that you have to learn to get along with during working hours. Add to this the fact that you will have to fit into a hierarchy at work – where everyone is aware of the pecking order – and you have a recipe for potential frustration, jealousy and conflict.

When you have found work that suits your talents and abilities the main requirements to feeling happy at work are to feel trusted, valued and supported. Without these conditions the possibility of dissatisfaction and conflict may arise. In this chapter we look at how to criticise colleagues, accept valid criticism, compliment colleagues, ask for promotion and say 'no' to unfair demands.

Giving criticism

" Criticism is something we can avoid easily by saying nothing, doing nothing, and being nothing. "

Aristotle

Peter and Ann both work for a training organisation. They get on well together and have recently been given a project to organise short courses for office workers at their workplace. Ann had worked hard all weekend on a presentation of their ideas to be given to the management team. She then had to brief Peter so that they could present the work together.

Their presentation was well received but Peter didn't give Ann the credit for it. He felt guilty because he felt that he hadn't pulled his weight on the project. After the presentation he simply said, 'Well, I think that went as well as could be expected. We'll have to wait and see if they take on our ideas.' Ann was annoyed but didn't say anything. She was irritable with other people in the office and made sarcastic comments when Peter spoke to her.

Ann is ambitious: she works hard and enjoys her job. She often takes work home and sometimes works late into the night and at the weekends. She can't understand why other people don't share her values. Although Peter is always charming and she enjoys his company, recently she is finding it difficult to work with him as she feels he doesn't do his fair share of the work.

Ann told a few other colleagues that Peter was lazy and that she had actually done all the work. She was reluctant to talk to Peter about it because she didn't want to lose his friendship or cause an atmosphere in the office. She did what a lot of people do when they are afraid of confrontation – she talked about him behind his back and was sarcastic when he spoke to her.

Treat others with respect

You have the right to request a change in someone's behaviour if it irritates you or upsets you in some way. However, you can still treat the other person with respect even when you are being critical. It is disrespectful to talk about someone behind their back; it can be cowardly and is certainly not assertive. Any annoyance or resentment that you try to ignore and push underground will undermine your relationship and will usually surface at some point.

"It is disrespectful to talk about someone behind their back."

Assertive *ACTION*

The whole situation might have been avoided by having a **frank and honest discussion** with Peter when he and Ann were first given the project. Ann could have pointed out to Peter what had happened in the past and asked him if he had time to work on this project with her. If there was no choice then it would have been better to get Peter to confirm what he specifically could and would deliver. Ann could have said: 'In the past when we have worked together I feel that you ... This time I'd prefer it if we sort it out before we begin. What are you prepared to do?' This needs to be said in an assertive – not an aggressive – manner.

If Ann says nothing to Peter she knows the situation will probably happen again. It is better to confront situations when they arise rather than letting them escalate out of control. **Gather together evidence before you criticise someone** so that you know that you are justified in what you say. When you have been irritated or annoyed for some time you need to plan what you are going to say – to avoid saying the wrong thing.

Next, **choose your time and place**. It is humiliating to be criticised in front of other people and it will inevitably cause a defensive or angry reaction. If you choose somewhere private you are much more likely to get an honest response. Think of how to cause the minimum amount of distress – by finding somewhere private and perhaps by giving a warning that they are not going to like what you are about to say. Put yourself in their shoes and think about how you would prefer to be treated.

Check your body language – don't stand too near or too far away. Make sure that your expression is relaxed and friendly – but not a misleading grin. Speak clearly and ensure that the tone of your voice is neither pleading nor sarcastic. Breathe deeply to calm yourself down before a potentially difficult encounter.

If you think it is appropriate, you can tell them first that you are anxious not to upset them. 'I've been worried about saying this to you … ' Don't forget the PNP sandwich: say something positive, then negative, then finish with something positive. So Ann could say: 'You know that I value your friendship but I feel I must say that your work on this project was … '. **Don't forget to criticise the behaviour and not the person** (so don't say 'lazy' or 'unreliable'). Once you have given your criticism, don't add to it with further abuse. Sometimes there is a tendency to become a bully – to enjoy the feeling of power and to want to keep on at the other person.

Give them a chance to reply at this point and don't expect them to be conciliatory – most **people react badly to criticism, even when it is obviously true.** You may hear some information of which you were unaware. Repeat this back to them: 'Do you mean that … '. The object now is to ask for a specific change. Just making a general complaint without suggesting an alternative won't help the other person to know what you want. Don't just hint, say specifically: 'In future I would like you to … '.

Notice that Ann does not mention the fact that Peter didn't give her the credit for doing the work. It's best to **criticise only one thing at a time.** Once you learn to be assertive you will also be able to let petty things go and not let them bother you. Save your energy for the important stuff. A good test of whether you should speak up is to see if it is still troubling you hours later. However, if you ever lie awake at night going over an injustice and what you should have said, then you must be brave and do something about it.

Finally, **talk about the consequences** – the positive consequences if they meet your request for change and, possibly, the negative consequences if they don't (it is up to you whether you tell them, but you do need to know in your own mind what you will and will not tolerate).

Remember

Specific and direct criticism shows that you value the relationship. Nothing will improve if you don't speak out.

Receiving criticism

Ann plucks up the courage to speak to Peter. She is nervous, but accuses him of lack of commitment and leaving her to do all the work. She does not mention the fact that he took half the credit for the work that mostly she did.

Assertive *ACTION*

When faced with unexpected criticism, the best way to respond is to **be as brief as possible** and then come back to the person later, once you've had time to think about it. So Peter could just have said: 'I need to think about this. Can we talk about it later?'.

Having had time to think about it, make sure that you understand what is being said. Paraphrase the criticism – so Peter might say: 'Do you mean you think I'm always doing this or are you talking about this one project?'. Once you have understood, then ask yourself whether or not the criticism is valid. **If you agree with the criticism, admit it** and say what you intend to do about it: 'I promise I'll do more than my fair share on the next project'.

If you agree with what they have said but can't think of what to do about it then **ask for suggestions**. 'It's true I am ... can you give me some ideas of what I can do about it?' If it's partly true then agree but qualify it. So Peter might say: 'I've had a lot on my mind lately and I admit I was more than glad to let you do most of the work. I usually pull my weight'.

If the criticism really isn't valid then say so. **Reject it firmly and confidently** – saying 'no' is powerful: 'No, that's simply not true'. Ask them to explain what they mean or to give an example. Begin your sentence with 'I' rather than 'You'. So you might say: 'I don't understand why you're saying that – can you give me an example?', rather than: 'You've got it all wrong'.

If you find yourself harbouring feelings of resentment about criticism, it is assertive to address it – even if it is days, or even weeks, later. Consider what has been said and honestly evaluate whether it has any validity. **Don't be tempted to refute criticism**

just because it is hurtful – but don't accept it just because someone else has said it. If you're not sure, ask them to rephrase it: 'Do you mean that you don't like … ?'.

"Consider what has been said and honestly evaluate whether it has any validity."

Whatever the body language of your critic is like (and it is quite likely to be antagonistic as giving criticism seems to make people either anxious or aggressive), make sure that you don't respond by mirroring their stance and tone of voice. **Try to relax your posture** (this is easier if you are sitting down), keep your voice low and speak slowly and clearly. Making constant eye contact can be aggressive, but do make occasional eye contact and don't look down or around the room. Watch that you don't put your hand over your mouth or pull at your hair (which shows anxiety), or fold your arms or point (this is aggressive).

If the criticism is constructive then it is assertive to **thank your critic**. Using people's names is assertive: 'Thank you, Ann, for pointing this out to me, I didn't realise … ' or, 'Thanks very much, I know I've … and I appreciate the way that you have discussed it with me'. Let them know what action you are going to take.

Remember

It will take some time for you to get this right. It's difficult for most people to respond assertively to criticism – particularly if it is unexpected. Don't beat yourself up if you react angrily, or tearfully – just learn from it.

Giving a compliment

Ann's manager was impressed by their presentation and suspects that Ann did most of the work. She doesn't say anything as she is not in the habit of giving praise or compliments to her staff.

In fact the manager was missing a great opportunity to show that she valued the effort and to thank Ann for the professional presentation. She knew that Ann must have done the majority of the work at home and that it was generous of her to include Peter in the presentation. Gratitude and compliments are an effective way of spreading good feeling – as long as they are sincere.

Noticing and commenting when someone does something kind, or thorough, or thoughtful, or careful doesn't cost you anything and makes the other person feel proud. Some people just aren't in the habit of complimenting other people, but everyone notices when someone does something good – it's just a matter of saying what you are thinking.

Not conveying these thoughts to the other person can be because you are not feeling good about yourself. If you find it difficult – ask yourself why. There is a generosity involved in giving a compliment and if you are feeling jealous or bitter or resentful towards the other person you may find yourself unable to pass on your appreciation.

Assertive *ACTION*

If you are going to compliment someone then **make sure that your compliment is specific**. Just saying 'That was good' is better than nothing, but actually selecting what was good and commenting on it specifically is worth a lot more. Ann's manager could have said: 'I appreciate all the hard work you did putting together the presentation', or 'I particularly liked the tone of the leaflet that you produced', or 'I thought the graphics were impressive'.

Giving compliments at work is an essential skill for a harmonious and productive workplace. Even when you criticise, it's best to find something good to say as well because then you will be more likely to be heard. **Be generous with praise and compliments**.

Quite often when someone surprises you with good work, or extra effort, or they relate a story in a clear and interesting way, the thought will cross your mind: 'This is really good, detailed work', or 'There's a lot of effort gone into this', or 'I can really imagine this happening'. Whenever you are aware of a feeling of admiration or appreciation, notice it and tell the person. Tell the shop owner that you like her window display; tell your partner what a careful driver she is; tell your friend you admire his honesty. You can begin doing this today – no training or practice needed.

Remember

Assertive people give compliments; it means you feel OK about yourself. Giving a compliment to someone else doesn't take anything away from you or your achievements. Be generous, honest and specific.

"Assertive people give compliments; it means you feel OK about yourself."

Asking for what you want

Megan, 50, is a social worker. She returned to the job after a career break when her children were young. Although she has done well in resuming her career, she feels that the work that she is doing far exceeds the original job description and that she deserves to be promoted to the next pay scale. She is assertive but still finds her manager can be difficult and unpredictable.

On the day that she has decided to ask her boss for promotion, she walks into the office and a phone is ringing but no one is answering it. She says 'Good morning' to her colleague James and he just snaps at her. There is a note from her line manager asking her if she could add one extra family to her case load. She opens her emails and sees that she has been asked to make a presentation to a visiting group of social workers from Sweden.

One of the reasons why we sometimes snap under pressure at work is because lots of things happen at the same time. It's much easier to be assertive if you only have one issue at a time to deal with. If, in addition, your home life is running smoothly, you get plenty of fresh air and exercise, nutritious food and always have a good night's sleep, you will be much more likely to be able to cope. However, the reality is that at work, and at home, we have to manage the best we can with problems as they arise – and things rarely happen one at a time.

If Megan was not confident in her own abilities as a social worker and if she had not learned to be assertive then she would probably rush to answer the phone. She would say 'sorry' to James (and wonder what she had done to upset him), feel upset about yet another family being added to her case load, and dread making the presentation. She would almost certainly have abandoned the idea of asking for promotion. Let's see how she actually handled her day.

Assertive *ACTION*

An assertive Megan walks into the office with a confident stride and a pleasant smile, saying, 'Sam, please can you answer that phone'. She pauses to make sure that he does. This is **a specific instruction addressed to one person** and therefore much more likely to be acted upon. If she had said, 'Can someone please answer that phone?' no one would have felt any responsibility to do so.

If, like Megan, you say 'Good morning' and someone snaps at you, then either ignore them or say, 'I can see that we'd better leave you alone today'. **Don't take their bad mood personally** and don't say, 'Sorry to have bothered you' (which could be either passive or sarcastic depending on your tone of voice). If you tend to apologise when other people are bad-tempered then break the habit now – it's not your fault that their life isn't going well. You could use humour, but it may be inappropriate if something really is wrong.

Megan looks at the note from her boss and decides that she is going to leave this for the moment and give herself time to think about it. Remember, **you don't have to act immediately** on every email and note that you read. Megan makes an appointment to see her manager. Even if it is not the practice at your workplace, always make an appointment when you want to discuss something important so that you know there will be time to have your request heard. While she is waiting, Megan reminds herself of her recent achievements and checks that she looks calm and confident.

Megan has prepared for this encounter by gathering together the evidence of work that she has done, beyond her original remit, in the past year. She has also saved emails from her line manager praising her work and letters from clients thanking her for her hard work on their behalf. She has gathered information about the case load of other social workers on a similar level, in order to compare how much extra she has been doing. It's a good idea to **gather evidence** like this when asking for more pay or promotion – you might not use it but it means that you have it ready in case it is needed.

Check your body language: sit up straight, perhaps leaning slightly forward, with both feet on the ground. Keep your hands away from your face and don't fold your arms. Breathe deeply and speak clearly and not too quickly. Make sure your expression is appropriate and make steady eye contact for short periods of time (at least 15 seconds). It may seem a lot to remember at first but it will soon become second nature.

Now say, 'I'd like you to consider this carefully before giving me an answer'. This stops your manager treating your request in a flippant manner. Then say, 'I believe the work I have being doing in the past year merits a pay rise/promotion'. Wait for the response and then briefly give the reasons or, if he appears negative, repeat what you said. Don't forget that it's highly unlikely that your manager will say 'yes' immediately. **Your aim is to state what you want and your reasons** – a good result would be if she asked for time to think about it. Finish by thanking her for listening to you, 'Thank you for this opportunity ... ', and arranging another appointment to discuss her decision.

Finally, **decide what you will do if your request isn't granted**. Megan knows that she can't afford to resign until she finds another job, but she has already found a couple of jobs on a higher pay scale. She has decided to apply for them if her manager doesn't agree to her request. It would be a mistake to say this – you are not threatening to leave, just promising yourself that you will look for a more highly paid job.

Megan returns to her desk and begins to prepare for the presentation. For many people a big fear is public speaking, and yet we are required to do this more and more often. Megan has done this before and knows that it gets easier with practice. It doesn't matter how nervous you are – how much you shake, sweat, go red – you won't die. The only way to overcome your fear is to do it. Megan sees presentations as a chance to show what she knows and understands. It will be useful in her bid for promotion. To calm your fears you need to **know your material, prepare well and practise over and over again**.

> ## "The only way to overcome your fear is to do it."

Remember

Many people remain in lowly paid jobs because they don't value themselves and daren't ask for a pay rise. There is no guarantee that you will get what you have asked for, but you will feel better about yourself than if you remained silent.

Saying 'no'

Megan decides that she can't possibly add another family to her already heavy case load. She is confident and capable and good at her job but she is also assertive and knows that she has the right to say 'no' without feeling guilty. Megan knows that her line manager won't like it, but she decides to tell her that she feels unable to take on yet another case.

It is often difficult to say 'no' when you are asked to do something. One reason for this is that people are afraid of the response that they will get – they are anxious about hurting the other person's feelings or, in this case, that the other person will be angry. Other people are afraid of being considered rude or selfish if they turn down a request. In some situations at work you may not have the right to refuse a job as it may be in your contract that you are required to do it. You do, however, always have the right to state the problems that the request will cause for you. You must then try to negotiate an outcome that is acceptable to you.

Assertive *ACTION*

Before Megan made an appointment to see her line manager she gathered information about the new case she was being given. When saying 'no', always find out the facts so that you **understand exactly what is being asked and what the implications are** for you. Make sure that you are not saying 'no' because you don't have the confidence (for example, if Megan had said 'no' to giving a presentation it would have been because she was afraid). If you always say 'no' out of fear then you will never learn how to do it. Remember that if you are not sure you can always ask for time to think about it.

Megan's immediate reaction was that she would not be able to cope with more work. When she enquired about the case that she was asked to take on, she realised that she was right. In this case she wasn't saying that the family didn't need help – just that she wasn't the one who could give it. When you are assertive you recognise that other people have needs but you **acknowledge that your own needs are equally important**.

Once you have decided to say 'no', **make your refusal short and direct**. Do not be abrupt or aggressive but make sure that your refusal is clear by using a calm and steady voice. You can disclose how you feel first if this seems appropriate: 'I am sorry to have to say this but I feel unable to take on any more work'. If the other person tries to persuade you then attempt to slow down your pace of speech and use fewer words or just repeat the same sentence: 'I'm unable to take on any more work'.

When your refusal is accepted then you may wish to **offer an alternative or a compromise** – but be careful that you don't backtrack: 'However, I am willing to … '. End the conversation by changing the subject or moving away once you have achieved your aim.

Remember

In order to be able to say 'no' to a request, you need to believe that your needs are as important as the other person's. People who say 'yes' to everything often end up doing the job badly or taking time off sick.

Top tips

- It is difficult to be happy with the rest of your life if you do not find your work satisfying and fulfilling.

- It is important that you find a job that suits your talents and abilities but it is also important to feel that you have the opportunity to progress and to learn.

- Progress and learning happens in an environment where you feel your talents are appreciated and where you are confident you can ask for help when it is needed.

- If you aren't happy at work then address the problem, or find other possibilities, instead of just letting things slide.

- If you begin to stand up for yourself when you are unjustly criticised, ask for what you want, say 'no' to unreasonable requests and accept the praise you deserve, then you will be respected and feel valued.

- Don't use emails as a way of avoiding face-to-face confrontations at work; if the person works in the same place and you have an issue, go and see them.

- All the same techniques (for example, how to criticise and how to say 'no') apply to emails – but you have to be extra polite because the recipient can't see the pleasant expression on your face or hear your tone of voice.

- Always check before you send an email that you have addressed it to the right person, and don't copy other people in unless absolutely necessary.

Chapter

8

'Go the extra mile. It's never crowded.'

Anon

How to get good service

It's happened to most of us: you find yourself on the receiving end of poor service, sales pressure or bad workmanship. Trying to get things put right can leave you feeling stressed, upset and frustrated.

The main issues with getting good service are knowing your rights, deciding what you do and do not want and having the confidence to take control. In this way, you will avoid being bullied and feeling at the mercy of others who have more control and authority.

In each of the cases in this chapter, you will see how an assertive approach can make all the difference to getting good service.

Asking for what you want

Grant decided to have a real wood floor fitted in his living room. He ordered and paid for oak flooring from a local store. The fitter didn't turn up on the agreed date. He'd been double-booked. The sales assistant gave Grant a new date and the work was rearranged for the beginning of the following week.

Although the floor was fitted on the new date, it was not finished. Grant was told that the fitter had to go and attend to another job. It was another ten days before the room was completed.

One month later the floor developed a fault; it had buckled, rising along one section. Grant blew his top.

As a result of the negative outcomes of past experiences, Grant had learned to become helpless and resigned. He perceived that he had no control over events, so he was unwilling to even try to exert influence over situations.

To begin with, Grant failed to take control when he accepted the new date he was given. It was not the most convenient day for him, but because he didn't want to risk the floor not being fitted again, by insisting on a more convenient time, Grant resigned himself to the date he was given.

The same thing happened with getting the floor finished. Instead of insisting that the floor was completed that week, by another fitter if necessary, Grant accepted the excuses he was given and waited another ten days. By the time the floor developed a fault, because he'd not asserted himself on the previous occasions, the fault was the last straw for Grant – a pressure cooker had developed and he exploded!

As well as allowing the situation to get worse, one of the main reasons people like Grant find themselves stressed, upset and at the receiving end of bad service is because they simply don't know how to say what they want in an assertive way.

It's time to make a change!

"People simply don't know how to say what they want in an assertive way."

Assertive *ACTION*

When you do not receive the service you expect, before you resign yourself to what you are told is or is not possible, **decide for yourself what you do and do not want**.

Once you know what you want to happen, simply and clearly state what it is that you do or do not want.

Start by using one of these openers:

- 'I would like'
- 'I need'

- 'I want'

- 'I must have'

Another effective way to get what you want is to **enlist the help of the other person**:

'I want ... How can you help me get that done?'

Or

'I need ... by the end of the week. Can you tell me how I can get that to happen?'

So, for example, Grant could have said: 'I need the floor fitted on Thursday or Friday this week. These are the only days I will be around to let the fitter in. Can you tell me how you can arrange for that to happen?'.

Once you have said what it is that you want, stop. **Stop and listen to the other person's response**. They may state that they can't do what you want. Or they may offer a course of action that you are not sure about accepting.

Rather than accept what the other person says can or cannot happen, if you need to, **take time to think through your options**. Simply say: 'I need to think about this. I'll get back to you'. This puts you in control instead of being subject to the other person's whims or at their mercy.

Accept that you may have to compromise. In some cases, the solution that you are seeking may be impossible. Grant's days off were Thursday and Friday each week. He wanted the floor fitted on one of those days. If he had told the sales assistant this, the assistant still would not have been able to have the floor fitted on Thursday or Friday this week, but he could have offered Grant Thursday or Friday the following week. Not a perfect solution, but better than taking another day's holiday leave.

Being clear and specific about what you want does not guarantee you will get what you want, but it does make it *easier* for other people to understand and meet your needs.

What could Grant have done about the floor developing a fault? Don't forget that **you have rights**. First, you have personal rights. If you believe you have a right to be treated fairly and honestly you will need to take responsibility for making that happen.

Secondly, you have legal rights. When you are in a dispute, whether it is with a shop, a tradesperson, a hairdresser or dry cleaner, know your rights.

"You have legal rights."

The Supply of Goods and Services Act 1982 aims to protect consumers against bad workmanship or the poor provision of services. It covers contracts for work and materials, as well as contracts for pure services. You can check your rights on consumer websites or visit your local Citizens Advice centre.

When things go seriously wrong, you will then have to decide whether to take legal action or, to avoid further stress, let it go and arrange for someone else to finish the work. This is an important aspect of being assertive – to know that **you can choose not to assert yourself**, and to take responsibility for letting go and opting for an alternative course of action.

Remember

You may not have got the service you expected, but by knowing your rights, what you do or do not want and saying so, you are in a better position to negotiate and get your needs met.

Giving criticism

Paula has started an Access course at her local college. She must pass the Access course in order to be offered a place on an Animal Science degree next year. Unfortunately, three of the students are becoming increasingly disruptive – arriving late, whispering with each other, interrupting other students, etc. Paula caught up with the tutor when he was on his way to another class and tentatively complained that she was finding it hard to concentrate in class because these students were distracting her. She hesitantly mumbled, 'Would you be able, maybe, to tell them to behave themselves?'. The tutor refused to take Paula's worries seriously, saying that no one else had complained.

Paula suffered in silence.

Paula found it difficult to make a complaint because she lacked confidence – she did not believe she had the ability to get something done. The tutor's attitude didn't help, either; if he had listened properly and treated her concerns with respect, Paula would have found it easier to assert herself.

As adults, it's very easy to fall into patterns that reflect what we have always known. Instead of standing up to her tutor, Paula reverted to schoolgirl mode – where the teacher was not to be questioned, criticised or contradicted!

Paula's lack of confidence and worries that her complaint would be dismissed or seen as troublemaking meant that she did not take her complaint further.

Assertive *ACTION*

If, like Paula, you are not used to standing up for yourself, the very thought of taking your complaint further might make you feel so anxious that you'd rather do nothing. But when you are assertive, the focus is not on how much fear and anxiety you feel, the focus is on **dealing with other people and situations despite your fears or worries**. Bear in mind that if you do nothing, you will still have to cope with the ongoing stress of the situation and the impact on your future plans. So feel the fear and do it anyway!

There are ways that you can increase your confidence in a situation like Paula's. First, **being more aware of and regulating your body language** can make all the difference to your ability to assert yourself appropriately.

Even when you are feeling anxious and worried, if you can master a self-assured posture you will immediately start feeling more confident. Try out your confident posture in front of the mirror and make yourself aware of what your confident stature looks and feels like.

"If you can master a self-assured posture you will immediately start feeling more confident."

Don't forget to speak slowly, audibly and calmly. Avoid gabbling – rapid and indistinct words confuse people and can result in your not being understood and the other person dismissing you.

Don't forget to **choose your time and place**. Paula made her complaint when the tutor was in a hurry – hardly the best time for him to listen to her! It would've been better to make an appointment to meet with the tutor.

Be specific about the problem. Paula made a generalised complaint: 'Other students are being disruptive'. She needed to add a specific example. In this case, Paula could've said: 'Today, three students were whispering and passing notes to each other. I found it hard to concentrate and learn anything in class because their behaviour was distracting'.

Decide what you do or do not want to happen and say so. The aim is to **ask for a specific change**. Just making a complaint without suggesting an alternative won't help the other person to know what you want. Don't just hint, be specific about what you want: 'If it happens again I would like you to … '.

If you are not happy with the response, say so and **say what you intend to do next** (it is up to you whether you tell them, but you do need to know in your own mind what you will do if your concerns are not taken seriously).

In this situation the college will most probably have a learning agreement. This will set out what students can expect in the way of a conducive learning environment and what the college expects from students' behaviour. There will also be a complaints procedure to be followed. Make use of these policies and procedures to support your case.

Getting the support of other people will also help you feel more confident about tackling an issue like this. Of course, you do not want to create an 'us and them' situation, but if you have noticed that other people also appear to be unhappy about a situation, don't be afraid to tell them how you feel and ask if they feel the same. If they do feel the same, ask them if they will be prepared to support you.

Remember

In order to feel more confident about making a complaint, manage your feelings, make use of assertive body language and get support from other, like-minded people.

Asking for what you want

Chris had an appointment at the doctor's; he was worried about a physical problem that had been recurring for several weeks now.

The doctor asked a few questions, carried out a physical examination, briefly explained the possible cause of Chris's symptoms and prescribed a medicine. At the chemist's, the pharmacist gave Chris the medicine, explained how to take it, the potential side effects to look out for and how to prevent or manage the side effects. Chris returned home and his wife asked how it went. Chris was vague – he had not understood what the doctor had said and couldn't remember exactly what the pharmacist had told him either.

Chris was frustrated – it wasn't his fault, he told his wife: 'The doctor didn't have enough time to listen. I couldn't work out what he meant when he told me what the problem was. The pharmacist was foreign – I didn't know what she was saying.'

Typically, people have problems with health workers because they simply do not have enough information, don't understand, misunderstand or forget what they have been told. They expect the professionals simply to get it right.

Often, we believe that there is a right and wrong way that others ought to behave towards us. We may expect too much and then, when they fail to meet our expectations, we feel let down, upset and resentful.

Most of the time, we are completely unaware of how our expectations can create all sorts of communication breakdowns, misunderstandings, conflicts and distrust.

Chris failed to ask questions and ask for more information, first because he did not expect to have to clarify what the doctor and pharmacist had told him, but also because he didn't want to show he hadn't understood; he was afraid of appearing thick or stupid.

Assertive *ACTION*

The next time you consult a doctor, nurse or any other health professional, prepare for the visit by writing down your concerns and current questions and what you want to know, before you go.

During the consultation, make sure you clearly understand what the doctor is telling you. **If you don't understand something, say so**. It really is that simple. Do not expect the doctor to know whether you have understood or not; ask questions until you feel that you do understand. Do not be rushed; calmly stand your ground until you feel you have the information you need.

Typical questions might be:

- What do you think is causing my problem?
- Is there more than one condition that could be causing my problem?
- What is the likely course of this condition? What is the long-term outlook with and without treatment?
- What is the medicine for and how will it help?
- Are there any side effects I should be aware of?

Do not be afraid to write down the answers, or ask the doctor, nurse, pharmacist, etc. to write them down for you. Of course, you are perfectly entitled to take a friend with you and they can support you by writing down the information you are given. Do not come away blaming the doctor for not getting what you want. Instead, you must **adjust your expectations, take responsibility and assert yourself**.

Remember

Never leave your doctor's office or the pharmacy confused or uncertain. Ask questions to clarify any uncertainty, and write down the answers. Take responsibility for getting the information you need to manage and protect your health.

"Take responsibility for getting the information you need to manage and protect your health."

Saying 'no'

Alex is looking for exactly the right shoes to go with an outfit she has bought for her brother's wedding. She has looked in several shoe shops but nothing has appealed. However, in the sixth shop Alex spots a pair that are exactly right. The sales assistant tells her that they don't have her size but they do have something similar. Alex tries them on but isn't sure. The assistant suggests another couple of styles. None of them is exactly right but Alex feels guilty about the fact that the assistant has gone to so much trouble and doesn't feel that she can leave without making a purchase. She agrees to a pair that are nearly, but not quite, right. Once at the till, Alex agrees to buy the shoe cleaning product as well.

Alex was brought up to believe that it is wrong to say 'no' to other people. In fact, if someone else appeared to be going out of their way to do something for her, Alex had been led to believe it was rude and ungrateful to turn them down.

Although, in the back of her mind, Alex knew it wasn't logical to have to submit to other people's pressure, she often ends up buying something she does not want because she gets stressed and confused and feels that the only way to leave the shop is to make a purchase and get out.

Assertive *ACTION*

There are a number of occasions where you might have found yourself under pressure to buy something – maybe because the salesperson has gone to a lot of trouble, or been particularly persistent. How do you avoid buying something you do not really want?

First, **notice how you feel**. If you are feeling uncomfortable or unsure about buying something, the message is 'don't buy'.

Don't feel guilty; you have done nothing wrong by not buying. Just because you ask the salesperson for assistance or information about a service or product, it doesn't mean that you owe them something in return for their time and hard work. If someone is in sales, they are going to have to deal with a lot of work and some rejection; it's the nature of the job.

Remember

Salespeople are trained to get you to spend your money, but you can resist them and there's a simple way to do it.

Just say 'No'. If the salesperson asks you if you want the item, just say that you don't if you don't. If you can't handle the direct approach, then say something like: 'Thanks, but it's not what I want' or 'I have to think about it!'.

They're not going to make a sale every time and you don't have to buy something just to please the salesperson. **What's important is that you're pleased with your purchase.**

Giving compliments

On the other side of the coin, people who work in service and retail industries usually work long hours and often for not a great deal of pay. If you have experienced good service, whether you buy something or not, show your appreciation. **Don't just say 'thank you' – say exactly what it was that you found so helpful.** Of course, if someone has really gone out of their way, make a phone call, write an email or send a letter to the company, explaining **specifically** what it was that the service person did so well. Your gratitude and admiration takes very little time and means that they're likely to maintain the high standards of service.

Remember

You have not done anything wrong by politely declining to buy something. Calmly decide what you do and do not want and have the confidence to take control. And if it's not what you want, say so!

Top tips

- Next time you find yourself fuming, stressed or upset because the service you receive is not what you expected or what you want, take a deep breath and assert yourself.

- Manage your feelings: do not think about how anxious you feel – focus on dealing with the other people, *despite* your fears or worries.

- Remember that in just about every situation you have rights, so get yourself informed and find out what they are.

- Calmly state what you do or do not want, listen to the response, then decide whether to negotiate and compromise or stand your ground and insist you get what you want.

- Credit where credit is due. The next time you receive good service, make a point of expressing your appreciation. Don't just say 'thank you' – be specific about what you found so helpful.

Chapter

9

'I don't think of myself as giving interviews. I just have conversation.'

Charles Barkley

'Death will be a great relief. No more interviews.'

Katherine Hepburn

How to be assertive at interviews

In the career development courses that we deliver, people often tell us that they find it difficult to assert themselves in an interview – to be confident and articulate. The main issues that they say they struggle with are:

- controlling their nerves and body language
- having to 'sell' themselves
- coping with a rude or incompetent interviewer
- being asked unexpected questions.

The ability to be assertive is an important factor in performing well at interviews; how you behave and communicate will be taken as an indication of how you will perform in the job.

Below, we examine the main issues associated with interviews and advise on how to behave assertively.

Acknowledge and accept your anxiety

Cameron had an interview at a publishing house in London. In the week leading up to the interview, he had become increasingly anxious. The big day came and Cameron sat waiting in reception feeling *very* nervous. The interviewer arrived and he limply shook her hand. As he followed her through the building to the interview room, Cameron talked nineteen to the dozen about nothing in particular.

Of course, there's nothing unusual about Cameron being nervous about the interview; most people feel this way. Cameron wants to get this job; he has put himself under pressure to do well in the interview so that he is offered the job. On the other hand, Cameron knows that he needs to remain calm in order to do himself justice. It appears to be a 'catch-22' situation.

Assertive *ACTION*

Cameron got off on the wrong foot when he began jabbering away before the interview had even begun. **Avoid waffling**, but do not think that you can make no comment on your nervousness for fear it will count against you. Instead, briefly admit that you are anxious but add a positive note – for example, 'I'm quite nervous when it comes to interviews but I am looking forward to finding out more about the job and the organisation' strikes just the right balance.

Speak fluent body language. With a handshake as limp as a wet noodle, Cameron gave a poor first impression. As soon as you meet the interviewer, extend your hand and give a warm handshake. Hold it for a beat as you look them straight in the eye, smile and say 'hello'. This is one of the simplest and easiest things to rehearse with a friend – practise until he or she feels that you've got it right. (And then you'll have the right handshake for every situation, not just interviews!) A firm handshake, a balanced posture, calm voice and gestures all help communicate an assertive approach.

Watch Barack Obama's body language. It is relaxed and fluid. It does not display tension or anxiety. He is calm and assertive.

To achieve the body language that's effective for you, focus on a single word and attribute – for example, 'calm', 'peaceful' or 'graceful' – and **practise carrying it out** in your movements on the day of the interview when getting dressed, eating, walking, driving, etc. It might feel strange at first, but it will help you feel and communicate the right mix of calmness and assertiveness.

When it comes to talking, note how Obama's voice is rhythmic. His voice emphasises certain words and draws them out.

He pauses frequently to allow others time to take in what he is saying. Pausing is a powerful tool. The person pausing lacks any fear of being cut off by the other person. So, speak up and say what you want to say in as **straightforward and calm a way** as you can manage.

"The person pausing lacks any fear of being cut off by the other person."

Remember

Instead of convincing yourself that you are not going to do well, tell yourself that you are going to have some nerves whatever happens but that you have little to worry about. You have nothing to lose (other than the job). There will *always* be other opportunities out there.

Know your limits and stand your ground

Jan is a hairdresser and has an interview with the manager of a new salon in the centre of town. The interview doesn't start well: the manager makes a dismissive remark about the last place Jan worked at, saying that it's a second-rate salon. Jan does not agree but is reluctant to say so.

It doesn't happen very often in interviews, but sometimes you catch people at their worst. If you do not agree with something the interviewer says, you have a choice – speak up or ride it out.

It's understandable that Jan did not want to contradict the interviewer, but as inadvisable as it is to get into conflict in an interview, you do not have to accept comments from an interviewer who adopts a sceptical, dismissive or even aggressive approach as a way of testing a candidate (or just because they are mean!).

There could be any one of a number of reasons why an interviewer was rude; at the very least, this is an opportunity to show him or her that you can handle an irate person.

Assertive *ACTION*

If the interviewer is being rude to you, speak calmly and get through the interview as well as possible. Chances are, if the person has a negative attitude you won't want to work there. But if you think they're just having a bad day, try to make the best of it.

If you decide to speak up, **simply explain why you do not agree**. In this case, when the interviewer was dismissive about Jan's last place of work, Jan could reply: 'I think that because that salon does not charge top prices, it's easy to think that it doesn't offer high-quality service. But actually, all the staff are professional, highly trained hairdressers with a regular clientele.'

If the interviewer persists, simply acknowledge what he or she said and **stand your ground by repeating yourself**:

'I know you are saying that someone has told you that it's a second-rate salon, but all the staff are professional, highly trained hairdressers with a regular clientele.'

If, however, you don't feel confident enough to calmly disagree, don't even try. If you choose to ride it out, simply ignore the remark; you can pretend you didn't hear it and just smile or stare blankly.

Don't forget, **you don't *have* to assert yourself**. An assertive person can choose to respond in a passive way and admit 'I am not going to react or do anything about it'. They may not like what the other person has said, but they recognise that they are in control by choosing *not* to assert themselves. On the other hand, if you do assert yourself, remain in control by calmly stating and restating your views and experience.

"Remain in control by calmly stating and restating your views and experience."

Remember

You do not have to accept rudeness from an interviewer – deal with it calmly and politely.

Asking for more information

Shula is being interviewed for a job as a nursery and sales assistant at a large garden centre. She has never worked in a garden centre before, but does have retail and customer service experience.

So far, the person who is interviewing her has done most of the talking and only asked questions that require Shula to do little more than answer 'yes' or 'no'. However, towards the end of the interview, Shula is asked a question that she doesn't understand. 'How do you think we can best help gardeners to adapt to climate change?' Shula mumbles something about not being sure that there was anything they could do.

Shula did not have the confidence to say that she didn't know the answer to that question. Although the usual advice may be to prepare yourself by anticipating the questions you will be asked, unless you have a crystal ball you are not going to know what all those questions might be!

Assertive *ACTION*

When it comes to handling a question you do not understand or know the answer to, the best advice to follow is to **be honest and say you don't understand** the question. It is OK to do this – you have a right to say you don't understand and to ask for more information.

If the interviewer is dismissive and says something like, 'Didn't you know that? You should, for this post', calmly reply with: 'It's not something I know a great deal about, but it sounds interesting. Could you tell me a bit more about it?'.

Whether it was a deliberate ploy or not, to see how you cope, **the way you handle questions you don't understand will say a lot about you.** In fact, it's possible that rather than being disappointed by your lack of knowledge or understanding, the interviewer may be more impressed with your ability to clarify and deal with the situation.

As well as questions you could not possibly anticipate, there will usually be other difficult interview questions that you *can* prepare for, such as, 'How have you coped in the past with difficult colleagues?' or, 'Why should we give you the job?'.

Simply type 'difficult interview questions' into a search engine and from the options presented choose one relevant to your interview that you can try out. Consider an appropriate response, based on your background and skills. Write down your answers. There aren't necessarily any right or wrong answers, but carefully consider the job you are applying for, your abilities and the company before you respond. **Do your research and prepare answers** to questions you might be asked.

"Simply type 'difficult interview questions' into a search engine."

Remember

Don't let tough questions throw you and ruin the rest of the interview. Be honest if you don't understand, and ask for clarification.

Identify your strengths and weaknesses

Chen is being interviewed by a panel of three people for a job in the press office of his local county council. One of the interviewers asks, 'Can you tell us something about your skills, strengths and weaknesses?'. Chen panics, thinking what am I meant to say? If I say what I'm good at they'll think I'm showing off and if I mention my weak points, aren't I giving them reasons to think that I'm not up to the job?

Being asked to describe your strengths and weaknesses is a text-book interview question. It is often asked because interviewers believe the answer provides, among other things, an insight into the candidate's level of self-awareness.

Often, people find it difficult to talk about their strengths and abilities because they do not want to be seen to be 'blowing their own trumpet'. However, a job interview is not the time to be coy and modest about your abilities; an employer needs to know what you're good at and what you can (and cannot) contribute to the job and the company. You need to prepare your answers to this question in advance, so that you can provide confident and assertive answers.

Assertive *ACTION*

Everyone can identify a handful of skills and strengths. It's a skill and a strength if it feels real – 'this is the real me' – and if you feel good when you use that skill or strength. It's definitely worth mentioning if it's a skill or strength that you can apply in this new job and it will enable you to do something easily and quickly.

Be clear and direct about what your skills and strengths are – expect to describe two or three. Crucially, you must **back up each skill or strength you mention with evidence**. For example, don't just say you have good customer service skills, prove it by describing what are, for you, good customer service skills – prompt attention and a friendly, helpful, interested manner, etc. – and then give an example of when you have used those skills.

What about your weaknesses? In Chapter 2 we advised that assertive people don't dwell on their weaknesses; instead, they learn from their mistakes and experiences. You must remember that nobody is perfect and that the interviewer knows that; he or she just wants to know any areas of weakness, **how you view your weaknesses and what you're doing about them**.

As with your skills and strengths, you must prepare for this question.

One approach is to take a skill or strength and also describe how it can be a negative. It often is, as we are all made up like two sides of a coin. Try it out with different qualities and accomplishments and see how it works. For example, 'I am persistent and see things through to the end. But this can sometimes make me impatient with others who do not work at the same speed as I do'.

"Take a skill or strength and also describe how it can be a negative."

Another approach is simply to pick a weakness of modest size – one that is not going to disqualify you from the job – and then describe what you are doing (or have done) to fix it. For example, you want to improve your spreadsheet skills so you are taking a course on that now.

Always turn weakness into a positive. If you lack experience or skills, for example, state this but also say that you are willing to learn, or that it is an area in which you would like to improve. For example: 'I do not have much experience with customer service, but I would like to be more involved in this. I get along well with people, I am able to listen and am a good communicator, so I feel that I would get on well in a customer-focused environment.'

Remember

Be prepared! Make a list of your strengths and weaknesses as they relate to the position, well before your interview. Everyone has skills and strengths. Demonstrate what they are the assertive way – honestly and clearly.

Top tips

- The ability to be assertive is an important factor in performing well at interviews. Employers will assume that your conduct during the interview will be the same conduct you will exhibit in the job.

- Preparation is key; research the company and the questions you are likely to be asked. Don't forget to practise assertive body language.

- Behaving assertively will help you to come across as a confident, capable candidate who is likely to get on with other people and be able to get things done.

Chapter

10

'I don't do meetings.'

Karl Lagerfield

How to be assertive in meetings

How do you approach meetings? Do you take over? Or do you tend to stay silent even though there are things that you want to say?

Meetings **can** play a useful role in getting people together to make something happen. Too often, though, meetings drag on and no clear decisions are made.

Although the responsibility for organising and running a meeting lies mostly with the person conducting it, you do still have a role to play; you can make sure that something worthwhile has been achieved.

Manage your expectations and make a contribution

Ricardo is a part-time teacher at a local college. He dislikes attending the monthly tutor meetings – they are long-winded and confusing. People don't listen to each other, the meetings drag on and nothing definite ever seems to be decided. Ricardo doesn't say much – he sits through these meetings, occasionally huffing or puffing and checking his phone for the time, hoping the meeting will finish soon.

Have you been to meetings that get bogged down in detail or derailed by side issues? Meetings where you don't feel confident enough to express your views, where the same person appears to dominate the meeting and people constantly talk over each other?

Often, we believe that there is a right and wrong way that others ought to behave. When people and situations fail to meet our expectations, we can feel let down. Ricardo expects that a meeting – any meeting – should follow a certain order and protocol. When it doesn't he feels resentful and won't take part.

"Successful meetings are more likely to happen if you take responsibility for your part."

However, successful meetings – meetings where everyone gets a turn to voice their ideas and opinions and clear decisions are made – are more likely to happen if you take responsibility for your part.

Assertive *ACTION*

Doodling, looking at your mobile, huffing and puffing are all indirect and dishonest ways of expressing your feelings; it's passive–aggressive behaviour. If, like Ricardo, you have no choice but to be at the meeting, instead of sulking resolve to make it more worthwhile!

Go with a purpose – to discuss something, to learn something or to make something happen. If you're not sure if you'll have anything to contribute, take the opportunity to practise your listening skills. And if you find it difficult to sit still and listen, take notes; scribble down questions, ideas and insights.

Make a point of listening carefully to what other people are saying. Be alert for something that someone says that *is* of interest. Don't just nod or shake your head; speak up! Say, for example 'I'm interested to hear more from Jim. His idea sounds interesting'.

You can also encourage the quieter people to be more assertive by asking them for their response, ideas or opinion. Make sure that your tone of voice isn't aggressive and use their name: 'What do you think, Gina, about this …?'.

When you do have an opinion, a view or idea, don't keep it to yourself – say what it is. Speak clearly – don't mumble or rush.

If someone interupts, look at them, use their name (in this example it's Liam) and say politely: 'Liam, I'd just like to finish what I'm saying.' If someone else is speaking and gets interrupted, or someone starts another conversation to one side, say the same thing, 'Liam, can we just let Marianne finish what she's saying.'

Often in meetings, the person who is speaking can stray off subject. If this happens, very politely, without appearing confrontational, say 'I'm not sure how what you're saying, relates to what we're talking about. Could you explain?'.

When it feels that a particular issue or disagreement has dragged on for too long, propose an action that could be taken next: 'How about we ....' or 'Can we at least agree that ...'.

Taking part in this way makes it more likely that you will leave the meeting with a clear idea of what other people think and agree to, and what actions will happen next.

Remember

Instead of feeling resentful and blaming other people when meetings don't live up to your expectations, be assertive. Take responsibility for getting your needs met.

Build your confidence and self-esteem

Cheryl is a tutor at the same college as Ricardo. She often finds the staff meetings frustrating. Her line manager, Lena, rarely supports tutors' points of view and usually defers to the department head.

At the next meeting, Cheryl wants to discuss the increasing amount of forms and paperwork that Lena has created and tutors have to complete. Cheryl feels that much of the

▶

paperwork is time-consuming and unnecessary. However, she is worried about being assertive with her manager in front of the department head and the other tutors; she's concerned she could come across as aggressive.

The key challenge for Cheryl is how to be assertive with others at different levels of authority, and with an entire room listening.

Certainly, it's not easy to be assertive if you lack confidence, are concerned what others might think or feel that the other person may undermine or even ridicule what you say.

But one of the benefits of being assertive is that you do not let fear of conflict silence you; you say what you do and don't want, despite your fears and concerns. You do not feel you have to prove anything, but neither do you think you have to suppress your views. You are also prepared to take the consequences of communicating your feelings and wants.

Another benefit of being assertive that is relevant here is that, because the principles of assertiveness remain the same whomever you're talking to, you are able to treat everyone as an equal and respond to others as equals. Other people's status or position doesn't stop you from voicing your concerns. **You know that you are all as important as each other.**

"Treat everyone as an equal and respond to others as equals."

Assertive *ACTION*

Of course, it's normal to feel concerned about expressing how you feel and what you do and don't want. But, **rather than focus on how much anxiety you feel, put your energy and focus on what it is you want to achieve.**

As always, start by being clear what it is you do and don't want. Think about what you find acceptable and unacceptable but be prepared to be flexible. Knowing and showing that you can negotiate will win you the respect of others.

"Knowing and showing that you can negotiate will win you the respect of others."

Cheryl decided that although she wanted the form-filling to be reduced, she was prepared to negotiate on what was essential paperwork and what was simply paperwork that replicated information that had been gathered on other forms and documents. At the meeting Cheryl explained her concern and asked 'Can we streamline the paperwork? How do other people feel about this?'.

When you are being assertive you are open to other people's views, even though they may be different from your own. But this approach has to be balanced with the fact that, **whomever you're dealing with, you do have rights**.

Cheryl's job description suggests that she will spend two hours a week on marking and other admin, but she usually spends three or four hours.

Know that when you voice your concerns and deal with other people and situations assertively, *despite* your fears or worries, you are also developing your confidence and self-esteem.

Once Cheryl had clearly and concisely expressed what she did and didn't want at the meeting, other tutors spoke up. They too felt that the paperwork needed to be revised. The department head agreed to review the amount of admin that tutors were expected to do.

Feeling more confident, Cheryl politely pushed her point and suggested that the review of paperwork could be something they did as a team – tutors, line manager and department head together. To her surprise, both her line manager and the department head agreed to this.

Remember

When you are assertive you are able to let other people know what you do and do not want. You do not allow concerns about other people's position or importance to stop you from speaking up.

Asserting yourself allows you to feel in control and believe that there is something you can do to manage a range of people and situations in a positive way.

Be open to other people's views

Clive is a member of a local residents group. Every three months the group meet to discuss issues related to their block of flats – issues such as building and garden maintenance, parking, noisy neighbours, etc. Clive often gets wound up at these meetings – he tends to rant and becomes frustrated and upset when people don't see things his way. He feels that the other residents dismiss his views and block his ideas.

Although everyone receives the agenda in good time for each meeting, Clive doesn't read it or find out any information about the issues to be discussed. He turns up at meetings unprepared and ill-informed. He reacts to issues in a way that comes across as confrontational and argumentative.

The problem is, expressing strong feelings inappropriately may result in other people feeling threatened and uncomfortable and they may close ranks against you.

The good news is that there are ways to express your opinions and **ensure that your views and objections get heard and responded to.**

Assertive *ACTION*

Before you arrive at a meeting, make sure you have read the agenda. Ask yourself, 'Do I know what the point of the meeting is and what the issues will be?'.

When you have something to say – questions, ideas or information to contribute – be specific. **Decide what, exactly, your point is and give examples to back up your points or ideas.** Speak slowly and calmly.

Listen to what other people have to say. When you are being assertive you are open to other people's views and opinions, even if you know they are going to be different from your own. Yes, you have rights, but so do other people. This doesn't mean you cannot disagree, but don't be aggressive. For example, instead of confronting someone with the remark, 'What planet are you on?', simply state what you don't agree with, then explain why you don't agree and what an alternative course of action might be: 'I can't see that working because … what I'd suggest is …'.

Express your opinion using the word 'I'. Instead of saying 'You are wrong', say 'I don't agree. I think that …' or, 'I believe that …'. It also helps if you **express ideas in terms of suggestions**, especially when things are getting heated. Instead of saying 'We must …' or 'You should …', say, 'How about we …' or 'Would it help if …'.

Be prepared to compromise; it's not about winning every time. Being assertive means settling differences of opinion by mutual concessions. Aim to reach agreement by making these concessions.

"Be prepared to compromise; it's not about winning every time."

If you realise that you have slipped up and failed to communicate assertively, the best thing to do is to apologise. This at least leaves the door open for better communication next time.

Remember

You can measure the success of your exchanges with others by how well you have behaved. Even if others will not go along with your ideas and views, you can come away knowing you have managed the situation in an assertive way, rather than an aggressive and confrontational way.

Top tips

- Take responsibility for your part in a meeting. Instead of feeling resentful and blaming other people when meetings don't live up to your expectations, be assertive.

- Go with a purpose – to discuss something, to learn something or to make something happen. If you're not sure if you'll have anything to contribute, take the opportunity to practise your listening skills.

- Don't let fear of conflict silence you; despite your fears and concerns, speak up! You do not have to prove anything, but neither do you have to suppress your views. When you are being assertive you treat everyone as an equal and respond to others as equals. Other people's status or position doesn't stop you from voicing your concerns.

- When you have something to say – questions, ideas or information to contribute – be specific. Decide what, exactly, your point is and give examples to back up your points or ideas. Speak slowly and calmly.

- Know that you have rights but be prepared to compromise. It's not about winning every time. Being assertive means settling differences of opinion by mutual concessions.

Chapter

11

'Let's build bridges, not walls.'

Martin Luther King, Jr

How to help others to be assertive

Whenever two or more people with different needs and expectations are together, conflicts can arise. Helping someone else to be assertive requires a combination of communication, assertiveness, counselling and mediation skills.

Below, we look at how to guide the other person assertively into more constructive action in four different situations.

Help someone to say what the problem is

Laurel works in a busy office at a secondary school. In the last few weeks she has noticed that one of her colleagues, Abi, is 'acting funny' towards her. Abi appears to be avoiding Laurel. When she does talk to Laurel, Abi does not make eye contact and appears awkward and uncomfortable.

Abi's attitude and behaviour is confusing Laurel and creating a strained atmosphere in the office. Laurel wants Abi to explain what the problem is but she's concerned that if she confronts Abi, she'll provoke a row or Abi will retreat. Resolving the situation seems difficult or even impossible, but someone needs to break the stalemate.

The challenge here is for Laurel to get Abi to open up and be clear about what's bothering her and what she does or does not want.

Listening, trying to understand their point of view and indicating what you agree with all contribute towards helping the other person shift from a position of passive–aggressive resistance to being able to tell you why they have a problem with you.

Assertive *ACTION*

If Laurel had approached Abi, with hands on hips, and confronted her with 'What are you so upset with me about?', Abi may have felt she was being put on the spot and either reacted angrily (aggressive) or denied that there was a problem (passive).

One of the first steps in helping others to express their feelings is to **be honest about your own feelings**:

'I feel like there's something wrong and it's worrying me. I don't want there to be a problem between us. Are you upset with me or is it something else?'.

In this situation, Abi responds by mumbling, 'Well yes, you always expect too much from me'.

Sometimes the urge to defend yourself is overwhelming, but don't! **Your role is to help the other person explain how and what they feel**, so ask questions to clarify, especially if the other person makes a generalised accusation ('You *always* …').

"Ask questions to clarify, especially if the other person makes a generalised accusation."

Ask them to be more specific: 'I'm not sure what you mean. Can you give me an example?'.

Once the other person has explained themselves more clearly, check that you have understood: 'Do you think that means I …?', or 'Let me see if I'm getting it. It sounds like you feel that …', or 'So. Are you saying …?'.

Ask questions to clarify until the other person agrees that you have understood.

Agree where you can honestly do so. This helps to establish common ground – a good basis for problem solving. For example:

- 'I have to agree that I've been stressed lately and ...'
- 'I agree that I ...'
- 'You're right, I did ...'
- 'I must admit ...'

Up to this point, your role has been to enable the other person to assert themselves. Having initiated the conversation, asked the other person to explain how they feel, listened to their response and found, if appropriate, areas of agreement, **now ask the other person 'What would you like to happen?'**. This is a crucial part of helping the other person to be assertive – getting them to take responsibility for saying what they do or do not want.

Now that you have helped the other person assert themselves, you are in a position to respond. You may decide that you disagree with their point of view and stand your ground, or you may agree that you have behaved badly and apologise, or you may feel that there is room to negotiate or compromise.

Remember

Helping someone else to assert themselves increases the likelihood of a 'win–win' situation for both of you. Help the other person to describe how they feel. Listen and acknowledge their point of view and discuss possible ways forward. Having a 'we-can-solve-this-problem' attitude goes a long way in helping the other person to assert themselves and say what they honestly feel.

Help someone to say how they feel and what they want

Marcus's friend, Bill, is upset with his sister, Gemma. He complains to Marcus that Gemma often organises family get-togethers but only invites Bill to join them on high days and holidays. He is never invited to Sunday lunches or BBQs with Gemma's family and friends.

Bill is feeling increasingly resentful. He moans and complains to Marcus and says he can't talk to Gemma about it. He says she's his sister, she should know how he feels.

Marcus suspects that Bill is not invited because, at social occasions, Bill often drinks too much and becomes loud and overbearing. However, Bill also lives a two-hour drive from Gemma, so maybe Gemma thinks Bill won't want to travel that far. Rather than guess the reason, Marcus needs to help Bill stop complaining and, instead, assert himself and let his sister know how he feels. It will then be up to her to explain the reasons.

Assertive *ACTION*

When someone else has a grievance with another person, be as empathic and understanding as possible. **Strive to look at the situation from the other's point of view.** Do not dismiss their feelings by saying, for example 'Don't be silly' or 'You're over-reacting' or 'You're being ridiculous'. Comments like these only serve to infuriate or silence the other person. On the other hand, if you want to help someone assert themselves, avoid jumping in with advice and solutions.

Instead, the emphasis is on helping the other person express their feelings and decide whether to act on them. Simply acknowledge what they have said and that you have understood.

For example, 'So, am I right in thinking you feel left out and you can't decide if Gemma is excluding you deliberately or just forgetting to invite you?'.

Next, **help the other person be clear about what they want and what the next step might be.**

Marcus could simply ask, 'What do you want your sister to do?'.

Often, you will find that the other person replies by continuing to moan: 'Well I don't know. It's just not fair. I'm not saying she should invite me every time, but I can't work out why she does this ...'.

Again, acknowledge how they feel but repeat, 'What do you want to happen?' or 'What would you like to do about it?'.

Help the other person to be specific. The aim is to encourage him or her to see that, rather than moaning and blaming, by deciding what they want to happen next, they can take control of the situation.

"By deciding what they want to happen next, they can take control of the situation."

Remember

When you are helping someone to be assertive, avoid the urge to leap straight in and tell them what to do. Instead, use basic counselling skills. Listening, asking questions and restating succinctly and tentatively what the other person has said will help them to see the situation more clearly and give them the confidence to assert themselves.

Help someone to set limits and stand up for themselves

Nadine has noticed that her colleague, Ray, is being bullied by their manager, John. At first, Ray denies to Nadine that it's a problem, but one day, over lunch, he admits he's finding it hard to cope with the humiliation of being shouted at and having his work scrutinised and unfairly criticised in front of others. He asks for Nadine's help.

There are two issues that contribute towards Nadine helping Ray to be more assertive; both have equal importance. First, Nadine needs to help Ray to identify his limits, assert his rights and stand up for himself. Second, Nadine must support Ray by confronting John and saying what she feels about his behaviour.

Assertive *ACTION*

When someone is being bullied, the feelings of shame, guilt and hopelessness may cause them to deny there's a problem and remain silent. If, and when, they open up to you, be as empathic and understanding as possible.

Listening, trying to understand their point of view and empathising with their feelings all contribute towards helping the other person feel less isolated. Once you have listened to the other person talk about how the bullying is making them feel, help them decide how to deal with another attack.

To start with, Nadine can encourage Ray to decide what his limits and rights are. He might feel that he can cope with the criticism but he draws the line at being shouted at. Or, Ray might realise that it's the humiliation of being criticised in front of his colleagues that he cannot accept.

Nadine and Ray could discuss what Ray wants to say next time John shouts at him in front of other staff members, and offer to rehearse Ray's assertive response with him. (Not forgetting to rehearse assertive body language!) Encourage the person being bullied not to make accusations, but to use non-emotive language and stick closely to the facts. Tell them to deal with one 'incident' at a time, rather than trying to address every occasion when they've been wronged.

"Encourage the person being bullied to use non-emotive language and stick closely to the facts."

Having helped Ray identify his limits and what he will say to John about what he will or will not accept, Nadine needs to reassure Ray that she will also let John know that she doesn't like John's behaviour. **If you know someone is being bullied and you don't do anything to help them then you're helping the bully!**

Choose a time and ask them if you can talk about a concern that you have. Explain what you have to say calmly, simply and without exaggeration. Begin with 'I've been feeling .... I'd rather that you did not ...'. Tell them what you want them to do instead in future, and remind them of the company's anti-bullying policy, which protects employees' rights. Avoid confusing the issue with another issue and using examples from the past to illustrate your point. Using past examples can lead to distortion and manipulation since the other person is likely to have forgotten or remember it differently.

You don't have to tell them this, but it is useful to have already decided what steps you are going to take if the bullying doesn't stop.

Remember

> Helping someone else assert themselves doesn't guarantee that people will stop bullying them, but it does mean that you will have helped them say what they feel, what they want and what they refuse to accept.

> You will also have shown your support by speaking out. A bully cannot operate where there is respect and support from other people. Yes, there may be consequences, but being assertive and helping other people to assert themselves means taking responsibility for the consequences.

Help someone to be clear and specific

Simon's grandfather has Parkinson's disease. He has recently been admitted to a care home. When Simon visits him, his grandmother is in the room and is distressed. She tells Simon that the staff are not looking after her husband properly and she wants Simon to take her husband home. She refuses to discuss her concerns with the care-home staff and insists that Simon speaks to them for her.

Simon is worried but recognises that this is not the time to persuade his grandmother to assert herself; he can best help by acting as an advocate for his grandparents. What's important here is for Simon to comfort and calm his grandmother so that he can find out in what ways, specifically, his grandmother feels that her husband is not being adequately cared for.

Assertive *ACTION*

In a situation like this, the first thing to do is reassure the other person that you are there to help and support them. Acknowledge their concerns and feelings: 'I can see you're upset; you're clearly very worried'. Ask them to explain each of their concerns, one issue at a time. Simon needs to find out in what ways, exactly, his grandmother feels that her husband is not being cared for.

Whatever their claims, **your role is not to agree or disagree, but to help them explain their worries and concerns**. Ask questions to clarify, and suggest that you write it all down so that you can read it back and they can confirm that you have understood correctly. (You then also have a written record to refer to when you take it up with a member of staff.)

"Ask questions to clarify, and suggest that you write it all down."

Once you have discovered their specific concerns, **ask the other person 'What would you like to happen?'**. This is the crucial part of helping the other person to assert what they do or do not want, and to help them feel they have some level of control.

Check and confirm what they want by summarising what they have said: 'So you don't think Pop has eaten anything at all today? You want to know if he hasn't, why not? And you want a member of staff to sit with him at meal times and help him to eat. Is that right?'.

Be clear with the other person what you can or can't do. Simon can't take his grandfather home, but he can talk to the staff and tell them in what ways his grandmother would like his grandfather better looked after.

Remember

As an advocate for someone else, you represent their views, wishes and rights. It is important, therefore, to be sure about what exactly it is that the other person wants and does not want, so that you do not misrepresent them. Writing it down gives everyone an opportunity to establish what was and was not said.

Top tips

- When helping someone else to be assertive, avoid taking over with advice about what the other person 'should' or 'shouldn't' do.

- You do not have to agree or disagree with the other person. Your role is simply to help them express how they feel and what they do or do not want.

- Let the other person know that it's OK to feel angry or anxious, that they do not have to feel guilty but can take responsibility and gain some level of control, whatever the situation.

Chapter

12

'Life is a mirror, if you frown at it, it frowns back;
if you smile, it returns the greeting.'

William Makepeace Thackeray

How to deal with difficult people

The assertiveness techniques that are described in this book cover many difficult situations. But there are some people you may meet who remain a problem, despite your best efforts at being assertive with them. It doesn't matter so much if the people you find difficult – the awkward customer, the bad-tempered taxi driver or the unhelpful receptionist – are ones that you encounter only rarely. If, however, the person is a family member or a work colleague and you feel you are constantly fighting a battle with them, or waiting anxiously for the next upset to happen, then you need a strategy for coping. Otherwise, you will find yourself deliberately missing family get-togethers or dreading going to work.

It may be that you chose this book because there is someone in your life that you find 'difficult'. As with decision making, there is no short cut. You need to work through the assertiveness techniques described in this book before you can deal with difficult people with equanimity. In other words, when you are in the habit of being able to give and receive compliments, when you feel confident about asking people for help and saying 'no' without fear, when you feel comfortable giving criticism and can receive it without it upsetting you – then you are ready to deal with any difficult people in your life.

Assertive people rarely have problems with difficult people because they know how to remain calm and impervious to their moods and demands. You cannot change the behaviour of the person you find difficult, BUT it is possible to learn how to deal with difficult people so that their behaviour no longer has the capacity to irritate, disturb or upset you.

What kinds of behaviour do we find difficult?

- **Stubbornness:** people can perplex you with their stubbornness and inability to compromise; they refuse to accommodate any point of view other than their own.

- **Selfishness:** those who act habitually in a selfish or hostile manner, even when it has been pointed out to them how hurtful this can be; they can be aggressive, rude and cruel.

- **Needy people:** difficult people can be high maintenance in their need for your time and attention; they can be so absorbed in their own troubles that they seem to forget you are a person with your own life and problems.

- **Sulkers:** they may thwart your attempts at being assertive with them by sulking, remaining silent (refusing to cooperate in any discussion about their behaviour) or being secretive.

- **Negative people:** another kind of person you may find difficult are those who are consistently pessimistic – despite your best efforts to point out the alternatives.

- **Unassertive people:** people who try too hard to accommodate what they think you want and end up irritating you by being overly anxious and too eager to please; people like this are often insecure and it can take a lot of effort to get them to express their own opinions or needs.

The behaviour of people we see as difficult can be erratic and sometimes bizarre. They may not be difficult all the time, which can be confusing and may lead you to try to ignore the bad behaviour when it happens.

Why are some people difficult?

People display the behaviours described above because it works for them. They have learned over time that by behaving in this way they can get what they want. What they want may be to avoid feeling the pain of feeling foolish or being rejected. They have learned that behaving in a way that we would label 'difficult' has made people more careful with them. It may not seem logical to behave badly in order to avoid the pain of being humiliated or losing an argument, but these behaviours have been learned over a lifetime and can be seen in children who behave badly in order to get attention.

Remember: you can't change the behaviour of someone else – you can change only yourself. But you **can** change yourself and your reaction to their behaviour.

Start with yourself

It may be useful to notice how other people interact with the person that you find difficult. Do most people have problems with this person? Are some people able to deal with them or work with them harmoniously?

If other people at work have the same problem, then it may be possible to discuss the matter with someone in HR (after all, that's their job). Often, in the workplace, people struggle on in their own private hell out of a sense of shame, or misplaced loyalty, when simply telling someone else might solve the problem. One of the ways teachers survive at tough schools is by sharing their problems (about students or colleagues) and by referring them to the relevant person. Those who try to soldier on in silence often take a great deal of time off sick or end up handing in their notice.

> "It is very easy for a grudge to become permanent and then the relationship becomes forever 'difficult'."

If it just seems to be you who finds this person difficult, then you may need to **examine your attitude towards them**. Perhaps this person has crossed you in the past (perhaps by not giving you some information, or lying to you or passing on gossip about you)? It is very easy for a grudge to become permanent and then the relationship between you becomes forever 'difficult'.

The way to solve this is to forgive them. It is surprising how quickly things can be forgotten once you decide to do this and make a genuine overture of friendship. Decide **you are not going to let the past ruin your present** any longer, and that you are now a confident assertive person who doesn't let these little things bother you. If they refer to it, just be magnanimous and say, 'Let's forget it. I already have', and give a genuine smile.

It's worth a try.

Similarly, if you are the only one who finds someone difficult, you may need to check your own attitude or prejudice. It may be that you have a tendency to stereotype people, and the new woman who wears ridiculously high heels and lots of make-up is not your ideal colleague. So her high-pitched chatter irritates you and causes an atmosphere that is easily ignited because you have already typecast her. It takes a very honest assessment of your own level of intolerance to admit that you may not have given someone a fair chance. And, of course, people are sensitive to your attitude towards them and so the spiral begins.

Earlier we noted how sometimes the person giving criticism is guilty of the same behaviour themselves; similarly, we may find characteristics of our own behaviour in someone we find difficult. Or we may find we dislike people for no apparent reason; this could be because somewhere in our subconscious they may remind us of someone in our past who was unkind or abusive. Again, the only way forward, if this relationship is causing you some difficulty, is to **put aside your assumptions and to make a genuine attempt to get to know the person.**

You may react against this suggestion, particularly if you have already 'had words' or full-scale arguments. But **an assertive person is not afraid of feeling foolish, or being rejected, or swallowing their pride.** It's worth it, if it removes your own sense of discomfort at being in this person's presence, or if it leads to a more harmonious atmosphere. You've got nothing to lose by trying.

'Needy' people

Sandra is a fitness instructor in a local health club. She enjoys her job and is often asked to mentor new trainee instructors. One young woman, Mandy, has begun to monopolise her by always manoeuvring herself so that she works next to Sandra and then by talking to her incessantly throughout the session. Mandy has a lot of personal problems and Sandra feels uncomfortable, as she doesn't want to listen but doesn't want to be mean. She particularly dislikes the way that Mandy gets much too close to her and talks at her all the time when they have a break. Sandra feels sorry for her and is worried that anything she might say to Mandy will upset her and 'push her over the edge'. Sandra is beginning to dread going in to work and is thinking about resigning.

So what would you do? Needy people like Mandy seem able to ignore all the unwritten rules of social behaviour and do not seem aware of the messages given out by a person's body language. Sandra has tried to avoid eye contact and attempted to move away when Mandy gets too close. She tries not to react to the things that Mandy is telling her and does not ask questions or offer an opinion. But still Mandy persists. Sandra feels sorry for Mandy because she is a kind person who can't bear to hurt other people's feelings.

Assertive *ACTION*

Very needy people need to be given clear boundaries. This need not be done in an unkind way. Sandra could say at the beginning of the session, 'I'm sorry, Mandy, but I like to be able to concentrate on the exercises with my client, and I can't do this when you are talking to me.' This must be said in a clear and confident manner so that there is no mistake, but there is no need to be aggressive. If she had time, and wanted to, Sandra could add,

'Would you like to go for a coffee after work?'. If you feel you would be unable to say something like this, then an alternative strategy would be to have a word with your line manager.

If you have someone in your life who you feel is demanding all your attention and sapping your energy, then **sometimes there is nothing for it but to tell them so.** Practise beforehand so that the words you use are direct and clear, but allow the other person some self-respect. So, if a friend rings you every evening to tell you about her marriage breakdown, you can say, 'I know you are going through a difficult time and I want to help, but can I ask you to ring me on Saturday morning instead of the evenings? I'm finding it exhausting listening to you after a day at work.' (The last sentence might be too cruel for some people – it depends on your relationship with them.)

Remember

If you have a needy person in your life and they are beginning to annoy you with their high-maintenance demands, then it is crucial that you do something about it rather than simply opting out (by avoiding them or not answering the phone). Of course, there may be consequences: **people don't like it when you don't do what they want you to do** – particularly if they are used to you being compliant. They may decide they don't want anything more to do with you, or they may be angry with you and call you selfish. Remind yourself that you are an assertive person who is taking the responsibility for your own actions.

"It is crucial that you do something about it rather than simply opting out."

Negative people

Will has been married for three years, but finds his relationship with his widowed mother-in-law increasingly difficult. He has tried his best to get on well with her, but finds her negative attitude to almost everything and everybody is beginning to depress him and he has started making excuses whenever his wife wants to visit her mother or have her to visit them. He realises that he can't avoid his mother-in-law all his life and that his attitude towards her is beginning to put a strain on his relationship with his wife.

Negative people can be very difficult to deal with, because being with them can suppress your normal cheerful personality. Having a negative person in the workplace, or at a meeting, can really change the whole atmosphere and ethos (just as a positive person can, in reverse). Living with someone with a negative personality can be depressing, if you allow yourself to be affected by their attitude. And they can be hard work, if you are constantly on a mission to change them.

It is possible for people with a pessimistic or negative outlook on life to change – but only if they want to and work really hard at it. **It is not possible to change someone else and to make them look at life in an optimistic, positive way – unless they want to be helped.** You can, of course, cheer people up who are miserable or feeling down in the dumps. But we are talking here about someone whose permanent outlook in life is to have a glass that is half-empty (or even totally empty).

Assertive *ACTION*

Will's wife will probably already be aware of her mother's negative attitude to life and will have developed strategies over the years to deal with it. Will could discuss his problem with his wife and ask her for help in how to deal with his mother-in-law.

At work, watch how other people handle negativity successfully. As an assertive person, Will could sometimes say that he doesn't choose to visit his mother-in-law or that he is going to absent himself when she arrives. This doesn't have to be a row – just a personal choice when you don't feel strong enough to maintain your equilibrium. Negative people can be draining, and if you are feeling under the weather or a bit depressed yourself, this is not the person you want to be with.

"Negative people can be draining."

When negative people are complaining about their lot in life (or their neighbours, or young people today, or the state of the NHS, or the weather) **don't get drawn in to what they are saying**. If you try to argue with them, even if you can show you are right, they won't like it and will simply find something else to moan about. They are not going to say, 'Oh, you're so right. Why have I had such a negative view of the world all this time?' (or whatever you're dreaming of them saying). If you observe people who are able to deal with negative people, you will see that they do it by distancing themselves and refusing to join in the moaning with them.

Negative people enjoy the role of victim; they enjoy the feeling of being helpless against the horrors of the world. Unless you are a trained counsellor, you are not going to be able to argue logically with them; it is much more likely that you will get drawn into their world and, without thinking, you will find yourself adding to their list of grievances and things that are wrong. **You must protect yourself from this sense of futility by refusing to enter into the conversation** and remaining indifferent or changing the subject.

So the next time you are with someone who is moaning or complaining (and you can't get away), listen to them and say, 'I understand what you are saying.' Don't add, 'But I ....' as this will draw you into their world. Neither should you agree, nor say, 'You're right' – as this will again only encourage them to carry on. In particular, **do not get drawn into becoming their**

problem-solver or saviour – 'I'll go next door and speak to the neighbour about it.' Your aim is to be pleasant and detached, not to get involved in their cycle of moans and complaints.

If you have a close relationship with a person who tends to be negative, and they want to change, you could try asking them what would happen if they didn't do whatever they are complaining about. For example, if your partner was complaining about her boss: 'What would happen if you said you wouldn't work late?'. The reply might be, 'My boss would be furious.' Keep on, 'Then what would happen if you continued to say no?' They might say, 'I'd lose my job.' Keep on, 'Then what would happen?'. They might reply, 'I wouldn't have any money.' And so on.

The idea is that you are showing them that they do have a choice. When they can see that they are choosing to do something – that they are avoiding something unpleasant happening by the choices they make – then they can no longer play the victim. Again, **being in control of the decisions that are made and realising the possible consequences is all part of taking responsibility**.

Remember

This will help only if they want to be helped. You can't change anyone who is determined to have the same negative mindset they've always had.

Sulkers

Derek works as a sub-editor on a magazine, but he finds one of his colleagues difficult to work with as he seems to take offence very easily and can spend weeks hardly speaking to Derek. This creates an unpleasant atmosphere in the office and makes it difficult for Derek to do his job, as he often needs to discuss the work he is doing. When his colleague is sulking with him, Derek dreads going to work and is thinking of leaving a job that he enjoys.

Sulking is different to being quiet. It implies that some griev-ance has been done that the person resents, but is unable to confront. Living with a sulker or being the target of a sulker at work is one of the most difficult situations to deal with – even for an assertive person. **Sulking is a form of bullying and is a way of exerting control** when the person feels otherwise power-less. Sometimes, the sense of resentment can be so strong that the sulker will refuse to talk for long periods of time. This is seri-ous, particularly when it is between couples, as relationships can break down irretrievably when communication fails. In families with a sulking parent, children are often used as a go-between: 'Tell your father that …'. It upsets the whole family and implies to the children that it is acceptable behaviour.

Assertive *ACTION*

If this was someone that Derek didn't have much interaction with he could just ignore the behaviour and decide it was their problem, not his. When, however, it is someone he needs to communicate with every day and the problem is affecting him so much that he is thinking of leaving, then he needs a coping strategy.

If Derek has examined his own behaviour (as suggested previ-ously) and can see no reason or justification for his colleague's attitude towards him, then he could try asking for help from HR. Before doing so, he would need to keep a note of when and how often this has happened and the detrimental effect it is having. He would need to make sure that he could present the facts in a straightforward way, without whining or exaggerating. Again, there could well be consequences of his actions, but there would also be consequences if Derek continues to dread going to work.

Derek could also ask for advice from a trusted colleague who doesn't seem to have the same problem. **Picking up tips by watching other people's behaviour** is often how we learn to deal with difficult situations. **What he has to accept is that his colleague is not going to change; it is Derek who has to change the way he reacts.**

First of all, he has to avoid showing his colleague that he is upset by his behaviour towards him. The only point of sulking is to punish the other person – whether the slight is real or imagined. If Derek becomes quiet or depressed because of this person sulking, then **he becomes a victim and has allowed himself to be manipulated into behaving in a certain way**. Remember that, to begin with, being assertive is often like acting. Derek needs to stay calm and to check that his body language is not hostile and tense. He could decide that he finds his colleague's behaviour interesting and even amusing.

"To begin with, being assertive is often like acting."

Secondly, Derek must try to remain his own happy self with his other colleagues. When you are suffering because of someone else's behaviour, then it is difficult not to get dragged down and take it out on other people. This is not to say that he should adopt a false *bonhomie*, or a hearty laugh at everything people say, but just be his usual, pleasant, self-confident self. This may take some effort, if he is feeling stressed by his colleague's behaviour.

Next, Derek needs to look after himself. All these kinds of **problem seem much worse if you are feeling under the weather or not getting much sleep**. Derek may need to take a short holiday, or get advice from a doctor, so that he can return to work feeling refreshed and able to deal with his colleague's sulks and silences. He must make sure that his colleague is not invading his thoughts during his leisure time by practising banishing such thoughts and replacing them with positive ones. It is possible.

Finally, during a time when his colleague is speaking to him, Derek could try talking to him about the problem. This is what an assertive person would do and, as always, it would take some courage. Derek would have to **practise what he was going to say** and decide where he was going to say it. He'd have to **check his tone of voice and body language to make sure he wasn't being aggressive**. The best approach would be to suggest it is a joint problem: 'I'd really like to sort out the problem we sometimes have communicating with each other.'

Remember

Derek will have to listen carefully to his colleague and genuinely try to understand why he behaves in this way and ask him what he can do in future to avoid the same situation.

Top tips

- Examine your attitude towards them: make sure you are being fair and that you are not discriminating against them because of the way they talk or dress.

- Don't bear a grudge: if you have had a confrontation or difficulty with someone in the past, try to forget it – forgive and move on.

- Ask for help if you feel that you can't deal with this on your own, and learn from the way other people interact with this person.

- Try to distance yourself when 'needy' people try to monopolise you; don't get drawn in to their world by agreeing with them.

- Set clear boundaries for yourself about what you are prepared to do.

- When it is appropriate, speak to the person about their behaviour – it won't be as frightening as you think.

- Offer a compromise, if you want to (but you don't have to).

- Look after yourself and make sure you are calm and rested before any potential confrontation.

Chapter

13

'Destiny isn't a matter of chance: it's a matter of choice.'

W.J. Bryan

How to make assertive decisions

Like all the other skills of assertiveness described in this text, being able to make decisions will be easier in some areas of your life than it is in others. By now you will have realised in which situations you find it easiest to be assertive. If you are assertive with your family, then you are most likely able to make decisions concerning the family more easily. So, choosing a school for your children or where to go on holiday will not be a problem – because you are confident of your ability in this area. If, however, you are unable to ask for help or say 'no' at work, then it will be more difficult for you to make work-related decisions.

By practising the techniques described in the previous chapters, you will find that as you become more assertive you will also find it easier to make good decisions. In this chapter we will look at further steps you can take to help you with decision making by examining the dilemmas of some of the characters from previous case studies.

"As you become more assertive you will also find it easier to make good decisions."

The aim is to become more consistent in your reactions and behaviour so that you become confident about making decisions in all areas of your life. Whether you are the kind of person who agonises over every little choice, or someone who simply avoids making decisions by being passive, the good news is that it is possible to train yourself to become more decisive.

Differentiate between trivial and important decisions

" There is no more miserable human being than one in whom nothing is habitual but indecision. "

William James

We met Deborah in Chapter 6 having difficulty saying 'no' to her neighbour. In fact, Deborah finds it difficult to make up her mind in many areas of her life.

Deborah has many friends because she is easygoing and can usually be persuaded to go along with what everyone else wants. This is occasionally irritating as she rarely expresses a choice, and when asked where she would like to go she usually answers, 'Oh, I don't mind, wherever you want'. When they go to a restaurant together Deborah finds it difficult to choose what she wants from the menu. She deliberates for ages, asks everyone else what they are having and, after she has chosen, often changes her mind at the last minute. When the food arrives she invariably looks at someone else's food and says, 'I wish I'd had that'.

Similarly, when she goes clothes shopping with a friend, Deborah finds it difficult to choose. She often buys things without trying them on and has a whole wardrobe of clothes at home that she never wears. In fact, she wears the same few outfits most days – mostly black – not because she has made a decision to do so but because choosing what to wear each day is too fraught with anxiety.

Deborah was able to make decisions about her family with ease. Over the years, as a single parent, she had learned to be decisive about her children's needs and wishes. However, once they had left home and she began to develop her own social life with friends she found that making decisions was an area where she was more uncertain of herself. She irritated her friends, and herself, with her inability to make even the most inconsequential decisions.

Every day we make hundreds of decisions without realising it; some of these are unimportant and others may affect our lives, and those around us, in a profound way. The trouble is that we often agonise over the trivial decisions but make snap judgements about important things. To be able to make major decisions with confidence, it is first of all a good idea to learn how to deal decisively with the unimportant ones.

Assertive *ACTION*

To become a good decision-maker and gain more control over your life, you have to be able to **differentiate between the small decisions and the ones that really matter**. The way to decide this is to rate their impact over a period of time. Ask yourself: 'How long will the impact of my decision last?'. A one-star rating might be which film to choose. Two-star: whether to go to that wedding. Three-star: which university course to choose. Four-star: applying for promotion. Five-star: ending a relationship; emigrating; having a baby. (These are only rough guides of course; only you can rate your own decisions.)

If you are spending all your time worrying about trivial things, you will be unable to focus on the important ones. The five-star decisions that are worth your time and energy are the ones that wake you up in the middle of the night – the ones that will still matter to you over the years (these need plenty of time, perhaps months, of serious thought). When you give yourself time to think about something, make sure that it is productive thinking – not mindless agonising, going over and over the same ground.

If you realise that you use decision-making avoidance techniques about little things, **decide *now* to do something about it**. You might not be able to change the habit of a lifetime overnight, but there are some techniques that you could use to help yourself to change from being an indecisive person to one who knows their own mind. Begin with the trivial decisions that you make on a daily basis.

If you recognise that you have a similar problem to Deborah's, then you may need to **take action to help yourself become more decisive** about unimportant things. For example, if you recognise the problem she has with clothes, go through your clothes, sort out five outfits and wear one each day for the next week. Wear them with confidence and accept the compliments assertively. Determine not to buy any more clothes unless you first try them on (and always decide how much you are willing to pay before looking at the price). If you don't know what suits you, consider going to a colour analyst. They will give you a swatch of colours that suit you, and indecisive shoppers have assured us that it has transformed their lives.

If you **recognise your own behaviour** in Deborah's indecision in restaurants, then try finding out what's on the menu first (most restaurants have their menu online) and choose something before you go. Once at the restaurant, take a cursory glance at the menu and state your choice. Your friends will be amazed and you will begin to feel quite powerful and assertive. Whenever you are consulted about where you would like to go, or perhaps which film to see, try just choosing any – it is no more likely to be the 'wrong' decision than if you had agonised over it. It doesn't matter if the film turns out to be awful – who cares? An assertive person knows that trivial decisions just don't matter.

Once you have become used to making small decisions immediately, you will begin to feel more confident about yourself. The effect of doing this can be quite remarkable – particularly if you have always been someone who has dithered about for ages, never being able to make up your mind. You will find people will look at you in a new light and treat you with greater respect.

Remember

Get into the habit of rating your decisions on a sliding scale and giving them an appropriate amount of thinking time. Make all trivial decisions instantly; it will free your mind for the important stuff.

"Make all trivial decisions instantly; it will free your mind for the important stuff."

Make joint decisions together

"Take your life in your own hands and what happens? A terrible thing: no one to blame."

Erica Jong

Tiffany and Paul have finished decorating their new flat but they now regret their purchase as they don't like the area. Paul is a freelance graphic designer and works from home. Tiffany works for an insurance broker and has been dissatisfied with her life for some time. After a spate of burglaries in their area, Tiffany suggests that they move to the country and try to live self-sufficiently. Paul has doubts but goes along with the idea, and before long they have sold their flat and found a small cottage on the edge of Dartmoor.

When they get there they realise how isolated it is. Tiffany does not drive and the nearest village only has a post office and one pub. They miss their family and friends and realise that they have made a mistake. Paul tends to blame Tiffany as it was her idea.

This may seem unlikely, but in fact some people do move from a city to a rural location in search of the 'good life', before suddenly realising that the lifestyle isn't quite what they had imagined. (Liz Jones in the *Mail on Sunday* magazine writes every week about the disastrous consequences for her of making this exact decision.)

In this example, Tiffany made the mistake of thinking that she was being decisive, whereas in fact she was being impulsive. The difference between the two is the thought and research that goes into making a decision. It is easy to get carried away with your own, or someone else's, enthusiasm, but when it comes to the big decisions in life it pays to put some time and effort into exploring the idea before committing yourself.

Assertive *ACTION*

First of all, you have to be clear about the problem. Sometimes when people are unhappy they fail to **identify the real cause**, and set themselves on a course of action that doesn't solve the problem – because it was the wrong problem. Tiffany knows she is unhappy but it could be her job, or the flat, or the area, or her relationship. She seizes on the idea that moving to the country would be the answer without any careful analysis of what she actually wants in her life. If you have a major decision to make, clarify what it is and write it down.

Next, work out **what really matters** to you. Sometimes people make decisions based on what they think they should do, or what they think will impress other people. If you enjoy an active social life, shopping, eating out or seeing your family, then it would seem silly to move somewhere rural (but still people do it – and regret it). It's a good idea to write a list of ten things that you really enjoy doing – how does this list fit in with your decision?

If it is a decision that is going to affect others, then make sure that your decision is a joint one. Paul is as much to blame as Tiffany if the dream doesn't work out because he has passively gone along with her. **In a relationship, make sure that all major decisions are joint ones** – whoever had the idea originally.

Be flexible and consider various options. Do lots of research: ask around, gather information and visit the place at different times if you are considering moving. There are always more options than the obvious ones, but you have to keep an open mind and seriously consider them. (However, it is possible to be too cautious. You may consult everyone, read everything on the topic, change your mind frequently – until you have lost any remaining confidence in yourself and end up doing nothing.)

When you are **contemplating a life-changing decision**, try saying these sentences: 'This is something I really want'; 'I've thought long and hard about this'; 'I can really imagine what it would be like'; 'I've done lots of research'; and 'I've asked for advice before making my decision'. If you can honestly repeat these, then you are well prepared for the changes that are about to happen.

Finally, give your decision a chance – but don't be afraid to admit that you have made a mistake. No one is perfect, and making mistakes is the way that people learn.

Remember

Don't confuse being decisive with a tendency to be impulsive. If your decision is a joint one, make sure that both of you make that decision.

Ignoring a problem doesn't make it go away

"Few people have any next, they live from hand to mouth without a plan, and are always at the end of their line."

Ralph Waldo Emerson

Danny has money problems: he has a number of credit-card debts that are spiralling each month; he is behind with his mortgage repayments; and he has begun to borrow small amounts of money from friends. He deals with it by simply avoiding thinking about the problem; he tells no one and does nothing about it. His friend, Tom, has mentioned the fact that he doesn't pay his way, but Danny is afraid to tell him the real reason as he feels ashamed. He continues to go out with his friend but he is often bad-tempered or depressed.

He begins to feel ill and has started taking days off work. He is in danger of losing his job if he doesn't address his problem.

Danny may genuinely become ill, as people who are stressed often fail to look after themselves by eating well and exercising. Not being able to make decisions can be a major source of stress in some people's lives. You may have realised that your default reaction to most things in your life is to be passive. Making decisions might not seem to be a problem for you because you simply avoid making them.

The trouble with this attitude is that many problems don't go away until you do something about them. But just deciding to do something isn't enough – you have to make a plan and make sure that you carry it out. One reason why people waste so much money joining gyms is that they decide they want to get fit and so pay for a year's membership at a health club, they go a couple of times and then just let the idea fade away. In fact, they haven't really made a decision at all – they have just handed over the cash.

Assertive *ACTION*

Danny needs to make a **plan of action**. The first step is to work out how he got into debt. He could draw up an expenditure chart – detailing all his bills and outgoings. People are often reluctant to do this because they don't want to be faced with how much they are overspending. Once this is compared to income, the next step is to look at where cutbacks could be made. A debt counsellor can be a useful point of contact if your finances have spiralled out of control.

Although people are often reluctant to talk about money problems, **talking to friends is sometimes the best course of action** – otherwise you can find yourself losing them. Danny's friend Tom is annoyed by his friend's apparent meanness and has no idea why he is behaving like this. He may not be able to help, but just talking about it might encourage Danny to be more decisive.

After seeing the picture clearly and taking advice, Danny will have **various options**. For most people, money problems are solved either by spending less or earning more (or sometimes a combination of the two). Danny finds out that he can do over-time at work. His debt counsellor advises that he write to the credit-card company and his mortgage provider to explain the situation and agree smaller fixed repayments. He also cuts up his credit cards (it's often too much of a temptation to keep them) and controls his previous drinking, socialising and shopping habits.

A word of warning when asking for advice: be careful not to seize upon one piece of information or advice and give it dispropor-tionate weight. **Sometimes you hear only things that confirm what you want to hear** and you then discount anything else. So, for example, if someone suggests that you should declare your-self bankrupt that may seem an attractive idea, and you may then quickly discard the idea of debt counselling and being pru-dent for the next five years.

"Be careful not to seize upon one piece of information or advice and give it disproportionate weight."

Having made a decision to do something about a money problem, it is important to make sure that you **implement every-thing that you have decided to do**. Make a list of items and tick them off, one by one. If you keep a careful eye on your spending, you may find it surprisingly rewarding to see your debt going down each month. Don't forget to **monitor the outcome of your decision** – it can be easy to slip back into old ways if you don't keep a check on yourself.

Remember

Being unable to make decisions usually means we have little control over our lives. When we let things slide they usually get worse, and no one can help if they don't know about it.

Winning the lottery

When teaching assertiveness to a group of women at a local community centre, we discovered that ten of the twelve women in the class spent £5 a week on the lottery or scratch cards – despite the fact that most of them had money problems. All of them said that they didn't really think about it: they'd never made a decision to spend so much every week. None of them had ever won more than £10.

We pointed out that if they pooled their resources they'd have 2,500 chances of winning something by the end of the year. They decided to set up a syndicate, paying in their £5 each week and therefore being able to buy £200 of Premium Bonds every month.

We would like to be able to tell you that they won an enormous amount of money, but they did at least each have £250 saved in Premium Bonds by the end of the year. They all said that they felt more confident having savings instead of debts. For some of them, making that small decision was a turning point in their lives.

Use your head and your heart

" You don't get to choose how you're going to die. Or when. You can only decide how you're going to live ... Now. "

Joan Baez

David is aware of how his mother, Gloria, is becoming increasingly forgetful. She lives on her own and has few friends. Since her husband's death she has become dependent on David as he is single and lives much nearer than her other two children. David has started a new relationship but feels that his mother's health and welfare is his main responsibility.

Recently Gloria has started wandering the streets at night in her nightclothes. Her neighbours ring David and tell him that she is not eating properly and that they are concerned about her.

The biggest decisions in life can be divided into those where you are making a decision as a reaction to something that has happened (such as losing your job, someone dying, an unexpected windfall) and those where you are proactive and deciding to do something to improve your life (such as deciding to have a baby, moving house, leaving a relationship). In both cases you may need to combine your sense of intuition with logical deliberation. It's not a matter (as people often say) of following 'your heart or your head'; good decisions are often a mix of both.

The question of what to do with loved, aged and infirm parents is becoming increasingly prevalent. David realises that his mother can no longer live on her own but he is torn between the intuitive feeling that she would be happier living with him and the logical solution of putting her in a home. He knows that he cannot go on ignoring the problem as it is causing him sleepless nights and his mother is becoming a danger to herself and to others.

Assertive *ACTION*

As in all major decision making, the first step is to **understand the problem**. On the advice of his doctor, David takes Gloria to a memory clinic where he is advised that she is suffering from dementia. He is told that there is no cure and that her condition will, in fact, deteriorate.

You then have to **decide what really matters**. David wants his mother to be happy and thinks that, with help, he will be able to look after her, but he knows that it will be at the expense of his career and his social life. Could he live with himself if he put her in a home? He discusses the matter with his siblings: they are quite happy for David to take their mother into his home because then they wouldn't have to sell Gloria's house to pay for residential home fees.

The next step is to **consider the options**. David contacts various organisations – both private and National Health – to find out what help is available if his mother did come to live with him. He also visits various institutions to discover what they are actually like and how much they cost. He finds out that he doesn't have to sell his mother's home – he could rent it out, and that, together with her pensions, would nearly cover the costs. If he chooses the local authority home they are prepared to let the costs accrue until Gloria died and then they would take the amount owing from the proceeds of the sale of her house.

When you have done your research and considered all possible options, then is the time to **weigh up the pros and the cons**. You can write a list in two columns or give each option a star rating – anything that makes you give it some serious thought. Consider the possible consequences of each course of action, but don't fall into the trap of only thinking of the worst – think of positive outcomes too.

Making a serious decision takes **time, reflection and thought**. If there is any way to try something out before making a decision, then leap at the chance. David has his mother to stay with him for two weeks and the home he has chosen also allows her to stay there on a trial basis for two weeks. At the end of the trial period David can see that his mother is happier and more secure in the home. His siblings are glad that their inheritance isn't going to be affected, but David is just pleased that it is near enough for him to be able to visit.

In the end, **implement your decision** but don't forget to **monitor the outcome**. David keeps a careful check on his mother's welfare and is prepared to admit he has made a mistake and to change his mind if his mother doesn't seem happy.

Remember

Major decisions take courage: courage to take the risk, courage to act and courage to face the consequences.

"Major decisions take courage."

Get rid of the anxiety and fear of making a mistake

“You might be right, you might be wrong – but don't just avoid.”

Katherine Hepburn

Moira has decided that she has made a mistake in allowing Rob to move in with her. He has responded to her efforts at encouraging him to take on his share of the housework by being absent from home more and more often. When he is home they are always arguing and she feels that it is having a detrimental effect on her children. She has noticed that he often takes private calls on his mobile and she strongly suspects that he is having an affair.

Moira can't decide what to do about the situation. She knows that if she confronts Rob it will result in his leaving and she is not sure that this is what she wants. She is worried about another upheaval for the boys and she has also become used to another income, which has made her life a lot easier than when she was on her own. She is becoming depressed but is afraid of the consequences if she speaks out.

One of the reasons why you might find it difficult to make decisions may be because you have become so used to deferring to the wishes of other people that you no longer know what you want. In your different roles as a partner, friend, parent, employee you may have got into the habit of suppressing what you would like to do in order to keep everyone happy. So being assertive is crucial to being able to make decisions.

Another reason why people are indecisive is because they are afraid of making the wrong decision. This fear can paralyse you. People adopt the philosophy, 'Everything will turn out for the best', or 'I'm a great believer in fate'. You hear people saying, 'Let's see what happens' or 'Something will turn up' – anything rather than taking charge of their own lives.

Assertive *ACTION*

Deciding to do nothing about a situation is fine – as long as it is a well-thought-out decision – not just fear of an unknown alternative. **Remember that if you don't take control of your life someone else will.** Staying with the status quo *can* be a decision – as long as you make it one.

In this case, Moira has other people to consider besides herself. Moira's gut reaction is that she doesn't trust Rob and that she should ask him to leave. However, she also knows that financially she will be worse off and that the boys have become used to having more clothes and computer games. It is often easier to clarify what the problem is if you write it down. **Write down your intuitive thoughts as well as the practical ones.**

Next, **work out what really matters.** Once she does this Moira realises that she managed before Rob came along and she will manage again. The boys don't like the atmosphere in the house and Moira's mental health is suffering because of her indecision. Having a fixed view of what she hoped was going to be a perfect family life for them is what is causing her indecision.

The next stage is to **gather information.** Rather than getting into rows and accusations, it's a good idea at this stage to go together to an organisation such as Relate. Here you will be encouraged to talk freely and honestly and discuss your relationship in a safe environment. The Citizens Advice Bureau is also a useful first step for advice about finances and to find out if you are eligible for any benefits. It is usually best to get professional advice before you make any major decision.

> "It is usually best to get professional advice before you make any major decision."

Moira has also confided in a friend, but since her friend is recently divorced she is not sure that her advice is impartial. It has long been recognised that people's decisions are affected by their friends' divorces, pregnancies, house improvements, holiday choices and so on. Nowadays, it is not only the actions of family and close friends that have an effect on our decisions, but also a whole range of social networks. Although it is a good idea to consult other people, always bear in mind that **they will have their own agenda**.

By the time that they have their first appointment with Relate, Moira has clarified her financial situation so she is no longer afraid that she won't be able to manage on her own. Her decision about her future with Rob is now based on her feelings rather than need for him. It can be difficult to approach personal problems in this way, but sometimes it is the only way to **stop yourself going round in circles** and getting nowhere.

Once you have considered your options and have decided which is the best, give yourself **time to think and reflect**. This may take months in a situation like this – but make sure that you are thinking and not allowing things to slide.

Remember

If we are passive, it doesn't mean that nothing happens – it means that someone else makes our decisions for us, or random things happen that force us in a direction we may not want to go.

Top tips

"You gain strength, courage and confidence by every experience in which you really stop to look fear in the face ... You must do the things you cannot do.**"**

Eleanor Roosevelt

- Understand the problem; clarify what the exact problem is and write it down.
- Work out what really matters; striving for something that doesn't reflect who you really are is a recipe for unhappiness. Accept responsibility and know that there is no right or wrong answer – or perfect outcome.

- Come up with various options; if you have one fixed goal you are setting yourself up to be unhappy. Be flexible: do your research, ask around, gather information – even if it doesn't support your preferred course of action.

- Choose the best option. Weigh up the pros and cons – write lists or give star ratings. Don't forget to consider the positive outcomes of each course of action. Use your heart as well as your head.

- Implement the decision but don't forget to plan how you are going to carry it out. Don't procrastinate at this stage.

- Monitor the outcome – check how it is going. You must give your decision a fair chance but there is no shame in admitting that you have made a mistake. Nothing is really a mistake if you see the whole of life as an opportunity to learn.

Conclusion

In a BBC Two programme (26 October 2009), Warren Buffett, the second richest man in the world (after Bill Gates), was asked by Evan Davis how he was able to make so much money and yet keep such happy and loyal employees. He said that when he was 20 years old he was terrified of public speaking but that someone recommended Dale Carnegie's book, *How to Make Friends and Influence People*. Buffett said that after he read it he made a decision to consciously put the book's advice into practice and that the decision changed his life.

By reading this book you too have chosen to start on a life-changing journey. Give yourself time and be patient with your progress – any form of significant change doesn't happen overnight. Go back and revisit areas that you find the easiest to put into practice and try giving yourself little challenges. Every time you overcome a fear and do something assertive, it becomes easier the next time.

Reading this book may not make you the richest person in the world, but it could change your life in a profound and satisfying way. Nothing quite beats the feeling of knowing that you are not afraid to stand up for yourself and other people and to go after what you want and what you believe in in life.

Being assertive means getting your priorities right and negotiating with other people rather than arguing. It means an end to worrying about trivial things and those sleepless nights going over what you should have said. Being assertive means being authentic – knowing who you are and what you believe in. It simplifies life and enables you to focus on what is important.

You've taken the first step towards a more self-assured life – keep going and, we promise, you'll never look back. Good luck!

Appendix 1

Useful assertive phrases and quick responses

Sometimes when you find yourself in a difficult situation it is not easy to think of the assertive thing to say. Here are a few ready-made responses and requests that might come in useful at some time:

- I find that remark offensive.
- I find your behaviour unacceptable.
- That's not like you to say something so mean/cruel/hurtful.
- I'm sorry you feel like that.
- I can see how you might think that.
- I don't understand – can you clarify that?
- That's an interesting question.
- I prefer not to answer.
- I'll bear that in mind.
- Where do we differ?
- I'm not sure what you mean.
- Point taken.
- No, I'm sorry, I can't.
- I'm afraid it won't be possible to . . .
- I would like to help, unfortunately . . .
- That doesn't work for me.
- I'd like to think about it.
- Can I get back to you later?
- I've thought about this carefully and decided that . . .

- I need your help to . . ./I need you to . . .
- What exactly do you mean?
- Perhaps we could . . . ?
- I am not prepared to . . .
- I understand your point but I am . . .
- I am concerned by . . .
- I have noticed that you . . .
- Can you give me an example?
- Let me give you an example.
- I feel angry/irritated when . . .
- I can see that you are angry . . .
- I am anxious about saying this but . . .
- You can say no to this but I wondered if . . .
- You're right: in future . . .
- What can we do about this?

Appendix 2

Courses and helpful organisations

If you want to find a course on assertiveness in your area try: www.hotcourses.com (which has a database of over a million adult learning courses in the UK – including assertiveness courses). Sue Hadfield and Gill Hasson (the authors of this book) also run assertiveness courses in the Brighton area. You can find information about these and other courses on their website: www.makingsenseof.com.

Being assertive doesn't mean that you know all the answers, and sometimes getting professional or specialist help is the best way forward. Below is a list of helpful organisations and their contact details:

Alcoholics Anonymous – support for anyone who wants to stop drinking (tel: 0845 769 7555, www.alcoholics-anonymous.org.uk).

Childline – a free 24-hour helpline with counsellors who will discuss any problem with children (tel: 0800 1111, www.childline.org.uk).

Citizens Advice Bureau – gives advice and helps resolve problems: legal, financial, etc. (www.citizensadvice.org.uk).

GOV.UK – official UK government website giving information about a wide range of public services and support (www.gov.uk).

Kidscape – aims to prevent bullying of young people and provides support for parents/carers (tel: 08451 205 204, www.kidscape.org.uk).

Mind – a mental health charity dedicated to creating a better life for anyone experiencing mental distress; click on 'A–Z of Mental Health' pages for a comprehensive range of information and advice (tel: 0300 123 3393, www.mind.org.uk).

National Bullying Helpline – covers all aspects of bullying, including instances at work (tel: 0845 22 55 787, www.nationalbullyinghelpline.co.uk).

National Domestic Violence Helpline – help and support for women experiencing domestic violence (tel: 0808 2000 247, www.nationaldomesticviolencehelpline.org.uk).

NHS Direct – a 24-hour confidential service offering medical advice and health information (tel: 111, www.nhsdirect.nhs.uk).

NSPCC – a national charity offering free 24-hour helpline for child protection and the prevention of cruelty to children (tel: 0808 800 5000, www.nspcc.org.uk).

Rape Crisis – support for women and girls who have been raped (tel: 0808 802 9999, www.rapecrisis.org.uk).

Relate – offers counselling, sex and relationship therapy (tel: 0300 100 1234, www.relate.org.uk).

Samaritans – 24-hour emotional support for anyone in distress (tel: 08457 90 90 90, www.samaritans.org).

Suzy Lamplugh Trust – offers personal safety advice and practical support (tel: 0207 091 0014, www.suzylamplugh.org).

Talk to FRANK – a free 24-hour helpline giving free and confidential advice and information about drugs (tel: 0800 77 66 00, www.talktofrank.com).

Index